Kitchen Detail

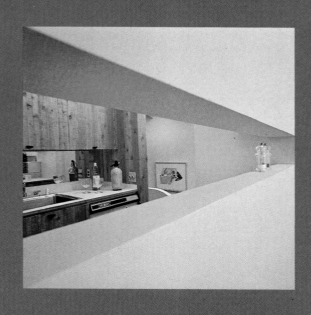

Acknowledgments

The enormous complexity that goes into the making of a volume such as this exceeds the scope of one person. It is my pleasure to share the accolades and tirades with a number of diligent associates who invested considerable time and effort behind the scenes. The food which appears in these pages was prepared by Cecile Lamalle. As you will see, she is a chef whose mastery is consummate. Those photographs not taken by me are the work of David Frazier. Neil Chesanow wrote substantial amounts of additional text. C. Ray Smith served as architectural consultant. Jamie Simpson was our chief spotter, tracking down foods, utensils and exciting photographic locales that are fresh, new and previously unseen. Emelie Tolley was our expert on kitchen equipment; she is as knowledgeable as any person I have ever met. Finally, KITCHEN DETAIL was designed by Joseph Santoro. His work on ATTENTION TO DETAIL, the previous book in this series, was nominated for a TABA award by judges of the American Book Association. To all of these people, I wish to convey my appreciation, admiration and thanks.

Kitchen Detail

Herbert H. Wise

With Emelie Tolley
Design by Joseph L. Santoro

quick fox

New York London

International Standard Book Number:
0-8256-3198-X (paperback)
0-8256-3204-8 (hardcover)

Library of Congress Catalog Card Number: 80-51628
Printed in Japan.

Distributed in Canada by:
Gage Trade Publishing, P.O. Box 5000,
164 Commander Blvd., Agincourt, Ontario M1S 3C7.

Cover photographs by Herbert Wise

Contents

Introduction

The Working Kitchen

Of all rooms, the kitchen has become the most essential. It is the one in which the most time is spent. It is the one on which we lavish the most money, even more than we spend on the average family car. The role it plays in the home of today is more vital, more varied, more public than ever before. The modern kitchen is more than a place for cooking and preparing meals. It is now a social center where family and friends gather to chat. It is the setting for dinner parties, a place for entertainment. It has been transformed into a workroom, a hobby center, for activities often unrelated to cooking *per se*. It is a place of hellos and goodbyes, the room in which we most often give our children a final approving glance before they hurry off to school and greet them when they return home. And the modern kitchen has become still more. It is now, in effect, a reflection of individual life-style and taste, a metaphorical last look in the mirror before we go out into the world to pursue our jobs and otherwise proceed with our lives. It has evolved into a dynamic, vibrant microcosm of modern life.

The evidence is everywhere one cares to look. Clearly, more people are turning their attention to kitchen detail than ever before.

But why? Why all the fuss over kitchens *now*, when the tasks of cooking and the need for a special area in which they can be accomplished have been an integral part of civilization, East and West, for a thousand years and more? The answer is both simple and complex: The world has changed. We have changed. The way we live our lives has changed. Our resources have improved. Our social conventions have been updated. Our concepts of food preparation and service and the role they play in our lives have undergone a subtle but significant evolution, particularly here in America. Slowly, quietly, we have drifted into a new era of culinary perceptions and experience, an era tailor-made for contemporary life-styles and tastes, an era of *New American Cuisine*.

One of the signposts of this era is our deepening preoccupation with health. Americans are jogging, swimming, playing tennis and otherwise exercising in

record numbers. Americans are dieting and giving up smoking on a grander scale than ever before. We no longer look upon three square meals a day as we once did. We no longer confuse satiation with being uncomfortably stuffed. We now consume less when we sit down to eat—and somehow manage to get satisfyingly full. We make an effort to eat better, more healthful foods. Our knowledge, our awareness has increased. The resources available to us have grown, and with them our desire for purity, freshness, naturalness and honesty in the cuisine we prepare and serve.

The cooking ingredients we now have at our fingertips are simply staggering. In the past decade, specialty food shops have multiplied and prospered. If a food or food product, if a seasoning or spice, no matter how rare or exotic, is grown or prepared anywhere in the world, it is now obtainable in the United States. It is now possible to enter a single store and find seventy varieties of sausage from which to choose, a selection of over forty mustards, scores of pastas and patés, over 400 meats, nearly 400 different cheeses and a great deal more.

What is more, we now have at our disposal a host of new labor-saving devices: food processors that can dice an onion or puree a potful of cooked carrots in three seconds flat; microwave ovens that can roast a lamb in thirty minutes instead of two hours; stove tops fitted with griddles and grills and special burners for woks; ovens that are self-cleaning; refrigerators that defrost themselves. Food preparation, cooking and cleanup were never easier than they are now.

But changing conventions of service helped to nurture and shape New American Cuisine as well. If you were dining in an elegant French restaurant around the turn of the century and suddenly had need of, say, a clean fork, your white-gloved waiter would swiftly deliver the appropriate utensil atop a folded linen napkin nestled in a small dish. He would never dream of touching the implement with his naked hand. With extreme deftness and delicacy, he would place it in its proper location in the table setting beside your plate. It must have been rather nice. However, the white-gloved waiter who is a paradigm of efficiency and decorum is a thing of the past. He no longer exists for most of us today, if he ever did. And so we have had no choice but to recast the classical French tradition of service into a uniquely American mold, one more compatible with modern needs and modern means, but a mold that is nevertheless intrinsically American: rugged individualism. We have had to learn to take matters, so to speak, in our own hands. But in the process we have made a rather pleasant discovery: The seemingly uncreative and menial tasks of preparing, cooking and serving food have turned out to be anything but. In fact, we have delightedly found that our involvement actually *enhances* our concept of contemporary entertainment, giving it a sense of relevance, of completion, of artistic participation that would otherwise be absent.

This yearning for purity, simplicity, honesty and naturalness embodied by New American Cuisine also extends to changing conventions regarding the preparation of the food itself. Much that the classical French chefs were trying to accomplish—the camouflaging of certain poorer grades of meat with thick, rich, elaborate sauces, for example—is not a necessity here, and never has been. For 200-plus years, Americans have enjoyed the finest meat available anywhere in the world. Even today, one can dine at a fashionable Parisian restaurant and find New York cut sirloin steak or roast Long Island duckling gracing the list of entrées. We have no need to hide our meat. We want to experience it fully: color, aroma, full-bodied flavor. We don't want it buried under an elaborate sauce, however complex and savory. This does not mean a sauce is an undesirable accompaniment to a meat dish; merely that it should complement the meat, enhance it, rather than disguise or overwhelm it.

New American Cuisine is not really new. It does not represent a complete break with classical French cooking. Rather, it is an evolution, an adaptation, a refinement, an updating to make it compatible with modern American kitchens, resources and tastes. It emphasizes the purity and excellence of ingredients used, urging that they be selected for their color, texture, freshness and taste. It

stresses "personal cuisine," with the accent on creativity and inventiveness but without sacrificing purity and simplicity. It seeks to recapture an unpretentious elegance in food which has, among the current practitioners of Escoffier's elaborate cooking tradition, too often been lost.

We have been transformed from kitchenophobes into kitchenophiles. We have become willing, eager participants in the cooking and entertaining process. We have cultivated a culinary sensitivity, technique, strategy, and depth of concentration akin to that of a professional tennis player homing in on an approaching ball, actually seeing its lines and texture while getting into position for the return shot.

New American Cuisine has changed the way we think about food. We plan our meals with meticulous care. We manipulate to make our courses work in concert. We want them to harmonize, to satisfy but not to overstuff. We set our tables with concern. We take pains and pleasure in making the dishes we serve look just right—as visually appealing as they are delectably palatable. We serve and attend to the needs of our guests with an enthusiasm that is genuinely felt. We are not merely satiating a collection of appetites. We are creating an event, an experience our guests will remember with pleasure. It is this total sensitivity to the entire culinary process that is the hallmark of New American Cuisine.

But the kitchen—the *American* kitchen—has also played a part in its development and widespread acceptance.

Throughout the world, the "American kitchen" is synonymous with the "dream kitchen." And for good reason. We have developed a technology of kitchen design and utility that has no contemporary peer. We have a greater variety of cabinet, countertop and flooring materials from which to choose than any country on earth. No other country has more different styles of kitchen design. No other country offers a greater selection of appliances, major and minor, to fit into those designs. We

have more space in our homes to accommodate them as well, something that even a technologically sophisticated people like the Japanese do not. Moreover, we live in a consumer market environment that encourages continuing improvements and ever-expanding variety. The "American" in New American Cuisine is no accident. It could only have happened here.

New American Cuisine is not a passing fad. It is here to stay. It has made cooking simpler, more creative, more exciting, a good deal more fun. It satisfies one's ego. It has metamorphosed cooking from a thankless chore that is taken for granted into a justifiable cause for celebration.

That celebration is what you are about to experience in the pages that follow. A sparkling array of new cookware and utensils awaits you. You will find fascinating sections on the ingredients of New American Cuisine—from eggs to cheese to fish to coffee and tea. There are illustrated procedures for preparing food, the proper methods for mincing, slicing, dicing, coring, carving and boning everything from a chicken breast to a rainbow trout. You'll discover a series of magnificent table settings in their appropriate locales that illustrate the scope of culinary experience encompassed by New American Cuisine—from a ranch breakfast to a holiday banquet to a country picnic to an intimate late-night supper for two. And, of course, there is a wealth of photographs of finished food—truly breathtaking meals —exquisitely prepared by a master chef, pictures that fire enthusiasm as well as delight the eye. For every dish portrayed there is a clear, simple recipe. Everything appears in rich glowing color.

But before we proceed to the art of New American Cuisine, we shall first explore the science underlying it, the architectural considerations for making the dream kitchen a reality in your home.

What Kind of Kitchen Do You Need?
There are five different types of kitchens.

The simplest is the *efficiency kitchen*. The concept behind it is that kitchens are separate places for cooks and that eating takes place in another part of the house, a concept at least as old as the first century B.C. The efficiency kitchen is small, basic, compactly designed for one cook and for easy cleanup. It is a closed kitchen with no open entranceways or passthroughs to other rooms, no eating counters or dining tables within, no space for activities other than cooking. While the efficiency kitchen lacks the counter space required by dedicated cooks, it does contain the essential equipment for creating the elegantly simple fare of New American Cuisine, providing the dinner party is small, six guests or less. It is the kind of kitchen often found in urban apartments, small

homes and, to a lesser extent, luxuriously appointed executive office suites. Of all kitchen types, it is the simplest, the most basic, the least frilly, and usually the least expensive.

Better integrated with other household activities are several types of kitchens which are less separate and which do incorporate open boundaries between cooking

11

and eating, nurturing a sensitivity to the entire culinary process that is the basis of New American Cuisine.

The *family kitchen* continues to be more than a room in which food preparation, cooking and cleanup take place; it is a primary social center of the home. It is, of course, an ideal kitchen for families with children. It is a good deal more spacious than the closetlike efficiency kitchen. While it is not necessarily open to other rooms via doorless entranceways, passthroughs or windows, it is nevertheless open within itself. In addition to facilities for strictly culinary pursuits, it generally includes a breakfast nook or counter (the most convenient way to feed children as they hurry off to school) as well as areas for play and relaxation when they are home. There is also a table where all regular meals (except, perhaps, dinner parties) are served. The family kitchen, you might say, is a combination kitchen and playroom or den.

A strictly contemporary development is the *entertain-in kitchen*, which extends the concept of the family kitchen to guests. It is designed not just for regular meals but for hosting dinner parties as well. As such, it is ideal for people who entertain frequently. The entertain-in kitchen is favored by confident, dedicated practitioners of New American Cuisine who want to share the delights of skilled food preparation with their friends and guests. It solves the problem of conversation between company and cook as the various courses are being created. Because the entertain-in kitchen is, in effect, a spotlighted stage, it must be more than spacious; it must be large enough to comfortably accommodate each member of the audience. Because it is the room in which the complete culinary experience takes place, it is generally the most opulent of kitchens. The floors, the walls, the dining area, the room decorations, even the lighting must be planned for aesthetic as well as utilitarian appeal; each must play a supporting role that complements and enhances the meals which are served. If the family kitchen is a combination kitchen and playroom or den, the entertain-in kitchen is a combination kitchen and living room or formal dining room.

A fourth kitchen type which is increasingly favored today as New American Cuisine continues to grow in acceptance, the *open kitchen* enables the cook to participate visually and verbally in conversation that is taking place in another adjacent room. Via passthroughs and operable windows (which are fitted with shutters that can be closed when privacy is desired), it is open to a living room, dining room, porch, pool, terrace or patio. Some cooks who favor open kitchen designs prefer them to be built on a raised platform that requires mounting a step when entered from an adjacent room. The slight elevation afforded by the platform sets off the kitchen space from the continuous plane of flooring running through the rest of the house, giving the cook a psychological sense of separateness from other rooms and guests while still enabling him or her to be part of the entertainment.

The most open of all kitchen types, the *hobby kitchen* is a direct descendant of early American kitchens common in colonial and pioneering times, which were large enough to accommodate the operations of spinning, weaving, sewing and knitting as well as cooking. Incorporating both family and entertainment activities, it includes provisions for several cooks—as well as flower arrangers, sewers, pottery collectors or other hobbyists—who regularly gather to pursue their pastimes in a setting surrounded by examples or collections of their hobbies which are generally mounted on walls or displayed on shelves. These activities do not occur in the primary work area of the kitchen, but rather in an adjacent area, away from the main paths of cooking. The *country kitchen*, in which antique utensils, implements, appliances—perhaps even a cast-iron pot-belly stove—decorate the kitchen,

giving it an air of warmth and nostalgia, is a variant of this type.

Which is these five basic kinds of kitchens is the right one for you? There are no easy answers.

A recent survey asked homeowners, most of whom claimed to be enthusiastic cooks, to itemize the requirements of their dream kitchen in order of preference. The results are revealing. Most said they wanted high-quality cabinets first, a separate pantry after that, a dishwasher next, and finally a self-cleaning double oven. All four desires indicate their primary concern was *not* with cooking *per se*, but with cleaning and storage. It underscores the importance of knowing what you really want. For only by realistically assessing your cooking requirements will you choose the kind of kitchen that works best for you.

There are a number of noncooking considerations as well.

For example, will your kitchen be a place for family and friends to gather and chat? If so, this has important implications for the space you will need.

Will you entertain guests in your kitchen? You will need a kitchen that is comfortable, opulent and atmospheric as well as functionally efficient.

Will there be children playing in your kitchen? If you have small children, perhaps you can plan for play space that keeps them safely out of the cook's way.

Will your kitchen also double as your laundry room? Some people prefer to keep laundering separate from food preparation because clothes washers and dryers can rattle unnervingly and bear no functional relation, except for plumbing runs, to other kitchen machines. Or they may simply want the laundry room or area located nearer the bedrooms, where most laundry originates and eventually returns. Others, however, do want the laundry room near or in the kitchen for the practical reason that it eliminates the need to install extra plumbing runs, one of the most expensive factors in any

room design. If you do opt for an in-kitchen laundry, have it installed near the plumbing runs by all means, but keep it separate from the culinary work centers, at least on a different wall or aisle.

Will your kitchen also double as your hobby room? If so, you must plan for space to work, store and display.

Will you plan menus in your kitchen, or draw up grocery lists, or work out food budgets, or pay bills? In this case you will need some sort of desk where you can comfortably sit down and concentrate.

Another space consideration is the size of your family, the frequency with which you entertain, and the number of guests you typically invite. If your family is large, if you prepare close to twenty-one meals a week, if you cook large amounts of food, if you find yourself left with tall stacks of dishes to wash, if you entertain regularly and your guest list is fairly large, you will need a kitchen with a large dining area and plenty of counterspace. If budget permits, you might want a heavy-duty, restaurant-quality stove, or an oversized refrigerator, or a separate freezer, or food warming areas, or perhaps two or more dishwashers. If, on the other hand, your family is small, if your dinner parties are irregular and of modest size, your spatial requirements and equipment needs will be considerably less.

How you want your kitchen to look is also a matter for forethought. The desire for an efficient kitchen that is easy to maintain tends to produce designs that are aesthetically similar from one home to the next—slick, streamlined, with the clinical look of a scientific lab. The cabinets, countertops, sinks and major appliances are gloss white. The visual lines are uniformly straight. The impression conveyed is one of automatic, machine efficiency. This minimalist environment is the norm for modern kitchen design.

On the other hand, the trend toward open kitchens brings other aesthetic considerations into play. Once the decision is made to expose parts of the kitchen to view from adjacent rooms, you must ask yourself if there ought

to be a consistency of atmosphere from one room to the other. Do you want your guests looking in from, say, a bright, warm, cosy living room or a flower-festooned porch to a cool, white, clinical laboratory of a kitchen? Or should the kitchen, if guests are somehow to be a part of it, be decorated to complement the other rooms? Do you envision your kitchen as a kind of backstage workshop, different in appearance from the lighted main-stage setting, or do you see them both as equal partners which should be similarly set?

The answer for everyone is different. A well-planned kitchen must work, must be efficient. It should also provide the desirable social and psychological milieu in which cooking takes place. And it should reflect the

attitudes, tastes and life-styles of its owners. Only you know what is right for you.

In new construction, the kitchen typically costs about 30 percent more than any other room in the house. In the 1980s, the average new kitchen in a metropolitan area set its owners back between $10 and $15,000. That's the middle-range figure. At the low end of the price spectrum, the speculative builder's kitchen—cheapest because materials, equipment and labor are purchased en masse—still costs a sizable sum: $4–$6,000 minimum. At the money-be-damned end, the custom-built architect's or designer's kitchen—which has the virtue of a tailored fit for each household—starts at $15,000 and often runs to $40,000 and more.

These are total costs. An itemized breakdown looks something like this: Major appliances average $400 each, with refrigerators ranging from $500–$1,800. Low-cost cabinets (the least expensive are plastic laminate) run from $80–$150 per linear foot width. A minimum extractor fan ducted through a wall (necessary for eliminating odors and heat) costs at least $250. Assuming you opt for the lowest overall kitchen cost, three to four major appliances will come to roughly $2,000, three to five cabinets from $600–$3,000, flooring material $2–$10 per square foot, and installation labor about $300 *per fixture* (including plumbing connections, electrical hookups, carpentry and lighting).

Of course, if you want the best, the price of everything goes up dramatically. Top-of-the-line appliances such as sinks with special faucets and restaurant-quality stoves will send the tab for appliances alone soaring into the range of $6,000 and up. Custom wood veneer and lacquered cabinet installations run from $250–$300 per lineal foot width, totaling $10,000-plus. With any kitchen, the highest costs are for the installation of electrical wiring, plumbing and ducting, for carpentry, and for the more opulent surfacing materials.

The choices seem difficult—even overwhelming—at first. Of course, we would all love to have the best of everything, but for most practitioners of New American Cuisine, that is neither necessary, practical nor economically feasible. Some compromise is needed. Self-analysis becomes crucial. Do you cook frequently or seldom? Do you prepare gourmet cuisine or relatively simple fare? Do you have special culinary interests that require special equipment? Will your kitchen be a social center for your family and friends? Will it be a hobby center? Will it double as a laundry room? When it comes to entertaining , will it serve as a backstage laboratory or a center stage? How much space do you have to work with? What will your kitchen needs be a year or two from now? How much money can you truly afford to spend? You must not let yourself fantasize about the type of cook you'd like to be and plainly are not. You must not envision the kind of life-style you'd like to lead and clearly don't. You must be ruthlessly honest every step of the way. Ironically, the surest guarantee that your new kitchen will start out as a dream and stay a dream is *not* to be a dreamer when you plan it.

What Kind of Organization Works Best for You?

A growing number of women who once had all day to spend in the kitchen now work. This social trend has stimulated architects, designers, manufacturers of kitchen materials and equipment, and research organizations to re-examine kitchen layout, to learn how the modern residential kitchen can be organized most efficiently with regard to the often decreasing periods of time available for preparing and cooking and for cleaning up afterward. As a result, kitchen planning has become a science. Recent time-and-motion studies have established new spatial standards which permit the most work to be done with the least effort in the least amount of time. Some of these standards are flexible; others are adhered to like unwritten laws.

The findings of this research are significant. They show that planning your kitchen with certain dimensions can save you 300 walking steps in preparing and serving breakfast, 500 steps in fixing dinner, and 450 steps in cleaning up afterwards. Your efficiency as a cook is improved. You use less energy in the kitchen, and you can spend less time.

Surveys show the kitchen requirement most often cited is working ease. To the majority of cooks, working ease boils down to three factors: There should be ample counter space to set things down—particularly hot cookware from the oven or stove—without breaking or marring the surface; the layout should keep the walking between work centers to a minimum; and the organization should eliminate the need for glancing around 180 degrees to find something or for moving some item—in a cabinet, say—to reach another.

While ample storage space ensures ease and quickness of locating what you need, sheer spaciousness alone is no guarantee that your kitchen will work efficiently. In fact, the overlarge work spaces in kitchens designed in the first half of this century frequently had a detrimental effect: because they required extra walking they caused extra fatigue. As a result, today's kitchen dimensions are calibrated by the most efficient pattern of work.

What are the basic activities you perform in the kitchen? They include storing groceries in refrigerator and cabinets; washing food; mixing, cutting, boning and other preparations; cooking; serving; eating; and finally cleaning everything up, which reverses the cycle. In a well-planned kitchen, each of these activities is most conveniently performed at a particular work center. Studies show that the three primary work centers center on the three major kitchen appliances: the refrigerator, the sink and the stove.

For maximum efficiency, the three major appliances are positioned in a step-saving triangle, regardless of the configuration of the room itself or the placement of counters and cabinets. The three points of the triangle represent the three most common tasks: removing food items from the refrigerator, washing them in the sink, and cooking them in the oven or on the stove.

In a well-planned kitchen, the refrigerator is never placed adjacent to the oven or stove, even if special insulation between the two seems to guarantee economical use and prevention of damage to each appliance, for it disrupts the efficiency of the triangular pattern overall. We shall see why in a moment.

In each corner of the triangle are preparation counters which provide convenient surfaces for work as you progress in the cooking process. Adjacent to the counters are cabinets for storing food items and plateware as well as locations for garbage disposal. Hence, every essential needed to complete a given work center is within easy reach.

What are the recommended ranges of distances for each side of the triangle? There should be 4–7 feet between refrigerator and sink. There should be 4–6 feet

between sink and stove. And there should be 4–9 feet between stove and refrigerator. In other words, the triangular work pattern, for top efficiency, should have an overall perimeter no larger than 12–22 feet. Some studies recommend a triangle that is even more compact: 15–20 feet in perimeter.

The Five Basic Kitchen Plans. Around the triangular work pattern, five basic layouts have been designed.

The *one-wall plan* is the simplest, smallest and least expensive of the five. It is ideally suited for the efficiency kitchen discussed earlier—where space is small, narrow

or otherwise limited. Here the triangular work pattern exists more in theory than in actual fact, as the three major appliances are installed along a common wall in a straight line. However, the three-step process of storage removal, washing and cooking is maintained. There are two disadvantages to the one-wall plan: It lacks adequate counter space for food preparation and service, and it lacks adequate cabinet space for storage. Nevertheless, it is sometimes the only kitchen arrangement possible. If your cooking interests are minimal, however, there is no need to plan a more elaborate kitchen—even if you can afford to do so. What is more, one-wall kitchens can be ordered as compact, complete, prefabricated units in a dazzling variety of materials. These units are easy to install and give you all the functional requirements of an elegant kitchen. Even for ambitious cooks with limited budgets or space, a compact one-wall kitchen unit provides the essentials for preparing a versatile repertoire of meals.

The next step up in size, efficiency and cost is the *two-wall or corridor plan.* Here the counters, cabinets and major appliances face each other from opposite walls and are separated by an aisle. The corridor plan offers a certain economic and utilitarian advantage over more elaborate plans: It does not require that cabinets be built into the corners where two adjacent walls meet. Such corner cabinets are costly to design and install, and frequently provide storage space that is inefficient because it is not easily accessible. Ideally, there should be no through traffic in a corridor kitchen, for it disrupts the efficiency of the triangular work pattern. Some designers recommend a minimum of 48–54 inches for the width of the aisle separating the two wall elements, but for kitchens in which only one cook will work at a time, an aisle that is 24–30 inches wide will do. It is recommended that corridor kitchens be designed in rooms that are at least 8 feet and no more than 10 feet wide (to save unnecessary walking steps), but the two-wall plan has worked successfully—if, perhaps, just a touch claustrophobically—in brownstone apartments with spaces as small as 6½ feet wide. A problem with this narrower width: Two facing doors cannot be opened at the same time. Excessively wide aisles, on the other hand, reduce your working efficiency by exceeding the recommended distances between refrigerator, sink and

stove, forcing you to take extra steps each time you move from one to another. Stove and refrigerator doors, incidentally, should not face one another. The heat from the stove partially defrosts an open refrigerator and the cool air from the refrigerator tends to lower the cooking temperature inside an open oven.

If you have two adjacent walls available and want to open your kitchen to other cooks and other activities— from in-kitchen dining to hobby pursuits—the *L-shaped plan* is an ideal choice. Here there are several advantages. It provides continuous counter space for working and spreading things out—an important convenience. It enables noncooking activities to be performed on the two free sides of the implied square plan. While the L-shaped plan provides no more storage space than the corridor plan does, it nevertheless ensures that there will be no cross-traffic through the triangular work pattern, another plus. It has, however, certain disadvantages. The L-shaped plan, by its very layout, often results in greater distances between refrigerator, sink and stove than are optimally desirable. And it does require at least one corner cabinet that wastes space and is costly to install. The least expensive way to circumvent

unit is no more than 30 inches wide) should be at least 5½ feet long; and the side with the sink and dishwasher should be no less than 6 feet long. When one leg of the U-shaped plan is open to a space beyond, it becomes, in effect, a *peninsula plan*, but this is more a variant of the U-shaped plan than a separate, distinct kitchen type.

Finally there is the *island plan*, which some designers consider a variant of other kitchen plans. It has at its center a chopping block, table, sink or cooktop surrounded by an L-shaped or U-shaped kitchen arrangement. Entire kitchens can be islands, but this is rare. Of the five basic plans, the island is the most costly, due to pipe runs, ducts and electrical wiring which must be concealed beneath the floor or in the ceiling in order to reach the outer walls. Nevertheless, the island plan is becoming increasingly popular, surpassing the U-shaped arrangement as the most glamorous and desirable kitchen plan in America.

Regardless of the kitchen plan you choose, if the kitchen itself is to be either the family or the entertain-in type, you will need a dining area as well. A table and four chairs require at least 48 square feet of floor space— 12–15 square feet per person. Each chair requires 32–36

this problem is to fill or turn the corner with an overhead or base cabinet (or both) that is accessible only through an adjacent cabinet door (although this makes for long reaches and considerable groping to find what you need). A better (and costlier) solution is a corner cabinet, which is fitted with a lazy susan arrangement inside—shelves that spin around in a 180-degree arc to put their contents within easy reach. Crowding major appliances into the corner is not a good idea; it disrupts the triangular work pattern, making each side of the triangle too small to encompass the requisite counter space the practitioner of New American Cuisine invariably needs.

At the moment, the most popular, most efficient kitchen plan in America is the *U-shaped plan*. In this, each of the three major appliances is located on a different wall, an ideal arrangement that results in the shortest walking distance between each work center while still allowing for ample counter and cabinet space. The U-shaped plan also discourages cross-traffic through the triangular pattern, always an important benefit. This shares the potential waste and expense of corner cabinet installation; however, if desired, both corners can be used for appliances which are diagonally installed. While the U-shaped plan adapts to both large and small spaces, the middle wall—the base of the U—should be no shorter than 8 feet to permit doors on either facing wall to be opened at the same time with a clearance of 4 feet. The side of the triangle containing the refrigerator should be at least 4½ feet long; the side with the range (where the

inches of clearance from the table to enable its occupant to stand up or sit down without bumping into a counter or base cabinet nearby. The normal chair extends about 20 inches from the table when someone is seated on it, 32 inches when that person stands up. If you plan to serve from behind a chair, you will need 44 inches of space from the back of the chair to the nearest obstruction. Table and eating-counter depths range from a minimum of 15 inches for breakfast meals to a maximum of 24 inches for dinners.

Let's discuss for a moment each of the corners, or work centers, in the triangle pattern.

The refrigerator center includes not only the refrigerator unit itself but also adjacent counter space, space to be used for putting down groceries on their way from the local produce market or gourmet shop into the refrigerator or on their way out of the refrigerator to the sink or stove. This center should also include cabinet space for storing canned goods with other dry foods nearby. Glasses for chilled or iced drinks, mixing bowls, graters, salad bowls and molds, pitchers and so on logically belong here as well.

The refrigerator should be placed so that the door swings open on the side that does not block the counter; if the unit has double side-by-side doors which open near the center, the counter space should be next to the door opened least, usually the freezer door. Refrigerators are available with hinges on either side, so be sure to specify exactly what you want when you order.

Most refrigerators are free-standing units. You can order a built-in model through kitchen dealers, architects and designers, but not directly from a showroom floor. However, free-standing units can be designed into your kitchen space to look like built-in models by placing cabinets and trim around them and the expense of customized carpentry is considerably less than the cost of a customized machine. Make sure your refrigerator has adjustable shelves; you'll appreciate the flexibility in holding items of varying sizes. And make sure that defrosting is easy. While automatic ice cube dispensers

and ice-water taps are great, keep in mind that each requires a separate water pipe run and plumbing connection—an expense over and above the cost of the unit itself.

The adjacent counter space for unpacking or removing food should ideally be 36–42 inches wide.

Of all kitchen work centers, the *washing or sink center* is the one most often used and requires the most space. This should be located between the refrigerator and the stove. Here you will need at least 24 inches of counter space on either side of the sink, but 36 inches is preferable. One side should have a sloping surface to drain water back into the sink after washing the dishes, and to facilitate drying, even if you plan to transfer glasses and plateware into a dishwasher later on.

In addition to the sink itself and the counter space flanking it on either side, the sink center should include a dishwasher, garbage disposal unit and trash compactor. For cooks with large families or who are frequent entertainers, two dishwashers in one kitchen have become increasingly common. Garbage disposal units are handy devices to have, but for reasons of safety, they are recommended only when there is a double sink, and the disposal unit is in just one of the sinks. Trash compactors normally fit into a space 15 inches wide in a base cabinet below the counter, or a 12-inch-wide space elsewhere. A compactor will fit into this space without

any additional carpentry or electrical hookups. The unit plugs into a standard duplex AC outlet. Storage space for sponges and the like should be nearby, within easy reach.

Sinks are available in a variety of elegant, durable materials—from gleaming stainless steel to the new Corian, a continuous surface material that looks like opulent marble and lasts like rugged stainless steel. The popular look among some designers is one of nostalgia for the kitchens of yesteryear. In increasing numbers, they are incorporating the once-common soapstone—or chemistry laboratory—sinks into their kitchen designs, as much for the exciting ranges of colors and textures now available as for their durability. Richly appointed with handsome faucets, available with a variety of mixing and spraying arrangements, they transform the sink center into an aesthetic complement to the kitchen as a whole.

The cooking center requires less space for cooking than for mixing, serving and other preparation on either side of the oven or stove. One side should have a heat-resistant surface so that hot pots and plates can be set down without damage. A marble pastry board can serve double duty here. But ceramic tile, stainless steel or other heatproof material will do the job equally well. Plate warmers are also best in this location.

Ideally, there should be 24 inches of counter space on either side of the range. To arrange food on six plates at the cooking center at one time and keep everything warm, you will need still more space. Cooking utensils, saucepans, skillets, casserole dishes, omelet pans, strainers, collanders and hand-held implements should all be within easy reach.

Choosing a stove depends on the amount of space you have for the cooking center, the place of cooking in your life, and of course, your budget. After an energy choice is made (gas, electricity or a combination of the two), you must decide whether you want a free-standing unit with a combined cooktop and oven or a separate built-in cooktop and a separate oven. Separate units are more expensive than combinations, unless the combined unit happens to be a restaurant-quality range. In addition, separate cooktops require more space than their combined

counterparts, so extra work space should be provided. Similarly, built-in ovens require a good 24 inches of counter space on either side for setting down roasting pans, casseroles, baking tins and cookie sheets that are piping hot. One alternative is installing a pull-out shelf above, beneath or near the oven.

Ovens are available with a variety of tantalizing accessories: self-cleaning systems, automatic timers, rotisseries, open grills, built-in griddles, special burners for woks and a good deal more. Which of these extras you really need depends on the kind of cuisine you like to cook and what you can afford.

The refrigerator, sink and cooking centers are the primary work centers of your kitchen. An additional center, the *mixing center*, should either be an adjunct to the refrigerator or the cooking center. It should have the largest working counter space possible, as well as adjacent storage facilities for dry food, mixing bowls, scales, measuring cups and spoons, pastry-making equipment, baking tins, wire whisks, wooden spoons, rolling pins and the like. Also within easy reach should be the mixing machine or food processor, hand-held mixer or beater, blender and electric can opener.

Ideally, the counter space of the mixing center should be fitted with a marble slab for rolling out pastry dough and candy, as well as a butcher block cutting board, both for preserving the sharpness of your cutlery and for providing a durable surface suitable for pounding meat thin with a mallet. Running widths of 36–42 inches are recommended, more if you have the space and the extended dimension does not excessively lengthen the recommended footage for the triangular work pattern.

Another secondary center, the *serving center*, provides space for platewarmers, either built directly into the countertop or resting on it as separate units. It also includes storage space for serving bowls, dishes, platters and tray. The serving center is usually combined with the cooking center, as at least some overlap is inevitable in any case. To comfortably spread out plates for food arrangement, a countertop width of 24–36 inches is convenient. If the serving space—or for that matter, if any countertop work space—must serve two functions, it is best to enlarge the area by an additional foot. Built-in, pull-out resting trays can also provide extra serving space.

enables you to wield a meat cleaver or a mallet comfortably. In addition, working a wire whisk around a mixing bowl is less of a strain when your arm is fully extended, as the 30–32-inch height allows, rather than partially bent, as the 36-inch height forces you to do. For similar reasons, a pastry board or marble slab for rolling out dough is most comfortable set at heights of 30–32 inches.

For built-in cooking surfaces, a height of 36 inches is the norm, but heights of 30–32 inches are occasionally recommended for cooktop stoves as well. To get an idea of which heights are right for you, measure the heights of your present counters with a ruler or tape measure and compare them with your general impression of working comfort when performing the tasks for which they serve.

Cabinets. There is a veritable cornucopia of kitchen cabinets from which to choose. They are available in every shape and size and in a dazzling array of materials. They can be ordered with a breathtaking variety of ingenious, convenient accessories. And they are expensive. In fact, cabinets are among the costliest elements of a kitchen.

Before you plunge headfirst into this high-priced consumer wonderland, ask yourself what at first may seem like a surprising question: "Do I need kitchen cabinets at all, or do I really need as many as I first thought." The alternative to cabinet storage is open storage: pots, pans, lids and utensils hung from a wall or an overhead rack; foodstuffs in canisters of glass, metal or colorful plastic neatly lining open shelves; wall-mounted or free-standing spice racks; plateware on visible display; and so on. Kitchen cabinets are convenient, yes, but a good many practitioners of New American Cuisine find that having everything within full view and easy reach — without having to open a cabinet door—is more convenient still. The visibility serves to remind them of the items thay need to do a given job. And the clean lines and sculptural look of the pot racks, canisters, spice racks, even plateware on the market today create an appealing decor in their own right. Of course, open storage does tend to use up the bulk of your wall space, no getting around that. But then, you'll never have the hassle of moving one item to get to another as you will have to do with a kitchen cabinet.

If you want cabinets in your new kitchen, you won't lack for exciting alternatives; they are endless, and each new one seems more tantalizing than the last. Manufacturers, responding to the trend away from

Counter Heights. Counter heights are often overlooked in planning a kitchen. The standard height for a kitchen counter is 36 inches, slightly higher than the standard height for a dining table of 29–31 inches. However, if you stand 6 feet or taller, you may want counters which are higher, or if you're under 5 feet you'll want lower counters. Chopping block and mixing counter heights are frequently lowered to 30–32 inches. The reduced height

clinical-laboratory kitchens to warmer, more personal cooking environments, have created porcelainized cabinets in a sparkling rainbow of colors and plastic laminate cabinets in rich, lush wood grains. The real innovations in cabinet design, however, largely result from the ingenuity of architects and designers who create new design standards for each customized job. One custom-designed cabinet system actually lifts off the floor to admit more light and air into the kitchen as well as reduce the need to stoop. Another employs tambour doors in the over-the-counter cabinets which slide up over the cabinet fronts and out of the way, just like the cover of a rolltop desk. There are still other alternatives. Cabinet doors, for example, can be made of transparent glass or clear plastic panels, offering closed but at the same time visible storage.

There is a rule of thumb for requisite cabinet space. It is 18 square feet for basic storage plus an additional 6 square feet per person. If you entertain frequently, add at least another 12 square feet of shelf space.

Upper cabinets are called wall units, while those beneath the counter are base cabinets. The standard base cabinet is 24 inches deep, with widths spanning 9–48 inches. Wall cabinets are usually 12 inches deep with heights of 12–48 inches.

Both wall units and base cabinets are available with adjustable shelves, pull-out shelves, lazy-susan rotating shelves, shelves that are wire baskets, tray racks, platter racks, half-width spice racks, and door-back racks for canned goods or whatever. You can also order pull-out units that can be wheeled into the dining room as a serving cart or flambé trolley or units that pull out to provide additional table space for breakfast. The wealth of kitchen cabinet designs, materials and accessories available is exciting, vast, ingenious. And expensive.

Lighting. The subject of kitchen illumination is considerably more complicated than it seems at first glance. Like the backstage of a theater, a kitchen needs overall work lights during the preparation of food and other tasks. But at performance time—New American Cuisine is enjoyed—the lighting must be of a totally different character: subdued, romantic, provocative, atmospheric. It should set the psychological tone for the meal; it should enhance the elegant simplicity of each dish; it should display with just the right emphasis, like a painting that is complemented by a well-chosen frame. Lighting specialists recommend that your kitchen be equipped with general, ambient or background illumination; lighting for work centers, major appliances and cabinet interiors; and accent or mood lighting for dining tables and ornamental displays.

There are two basic approaches for outfitting your kitchen with these three types of light.

The first involves keeping general work lighting and atmospheric lighting separate from each other. The usual overhead kitchen light, which illuminates the entire kitchen as well as counter drawers and cabinet interiors, is fine for food preparation, cooking and cleanup, but its

bright, harsh, factorylike glare is unsuitable for dining. And so it is balanced by a separate system of concealed-source lighting—beneath wall units or elsewhere—which provides efficient illumination around work centers. Recessed down lights fitted into the ceiling can also be used to spotlight work centers, but even they shed too much ambient or general light for dinnertime illumination; it is recommended they be hooked up to separate switches. In this approach, when dinner is about to be served, the overhead work lights are turned off and only the under-the-cabinet or otherwise concealed light source is left on.

The second approach involves aesthetic concerns. It regards exposed lighting fixtures—openly visible within the kitchen space either as bare bulbs or shielded shades of glittering glass or metal—as sculptural ornamentation. Nevertheless, for the same system of exposed lighting to provide soft dinnertime illumination as well as work-center work light, separate switches for each type of lighting should be installed.

Regardless of the approach you favor, rheostats or dimmers are optional—but convenient—refinements. They permit you to transform harsh work lights into atmospheric mood lights with a simple twist of a knob. In-kitchen dinners are but one meal situation calling for lighting that is subdued; buffets served from kitchen counters (even if actual eating occurs elsewhere) and intimate late-night suppers or snacks require an evocative romantic atmosphere as well. In urban apartments where the kitchen frequently opens directly onto the living room, permitting the harsh work lights overhead to shine into the eyes of the guests, some sort of dimmer apparatus is a must.

Similarly, accent lighting—which is used to highlight collections of things, either mounted on a kitchen wall or displayed on shelves—creates an air of beauty and drama that splendidly complements an in-kitchen dinner. These small, concealable lights are available in generous variety at any fine light store. Lighting with a strictly culinary function is provided by the infrared heat lamp, which keeps food warm on a countertop as it waits to be served. Hung from 13–18 inches above the warming surface, heat lamps keep an area 15 inches in diameter warm without overcooking or drying out the food. For saving energy by not leaving unnecessary lights left on, install an on-off switch at each kitchen doorway.

One of the trickier decisions of kitchen lighting is selecting the type of lamp or bulb you need, for the choices are not clearcut. Three types of bulbs can be considered: fluorescent, incandescent and quartz. Fluorescent tubes use less electricity, last longer, and produce less heat than incandescent lamps, but they also tend to produce a buzzing hum, especially when several tubes are used at once, which some people find annoying. If you do opt for fluorescent kitchen lighting, choose "chute" tubes for the agreeable quality of ambient illumination they provide. Incandescent bulbs or lamps use marginally more electricity, but they provide the most commonly recommended quality of general kitchen

lighting. They are available in a variety of decorative shapes that add an attractive sculptural dimension to a ceiling on which the lighting is exposed. Quartz or tungsten-halogen lamps use half the electricity of the others, last the longest, and produce an excellent quality of light for working purposes. However, they are also the most expensive to purchase, the most difficult to install and the most complicated to replace. They are not yet generally available for home use, other than through a designer or architect.

Today, the accepted norm for kitchen lighting is incandescent bulbs. Fluorescent tubes are starting to come back in vogue among yanguard designers who favor nostalgic kitchen atmospheres. Quartz remains the frontier—yet to be proven technically or aesthetically in the average residential kitchen.

Energy: Gas and Electricity. In planning your kitchen's energy systems, you must first decide whether you want an all-electricity or partially gas energy source. The choice usually hinges on the stove, although gas-fired clothes dryers are also available. Many cooks find themselves in a quandary when it comes to choosing stove fuel. Dedicated cooks tend to favor gas-fired stoves. They get just the amount of heat they want instantly, and they can control the heat better because they can see the burner flame and make adjustments accordingly. Electric ranges are cleaner than gas-fired appliances, but they take longer to heat up and are more difficult to regulate—for the degree of heat is marked on or near the on-off knob of the stove itself, rather than being visible to the-eye. Overheating for example, is a frequent problem as a result. Gas is cheaper; electricity is safer. (Even if you install a complete electrical system yourself, experts recommend, urge and caution that a gas system should be installed only by an experienced pro.) Some gas ranges can duplicate the consistency of heat produced by the old coal-fuel stoves, which has its advantages in certain kinds of cooking, but this is generally a special capability rather than a standard feature.

Electric ovens, on the other hand, produce constant, even heat, the kind of heat generated by brick ovens common in the nineteenth and early twentieth centuries, a desirable attribute. Electric microwave ovens, praised for their speed of cooking and electrical economy, cannot produce the browning effects of a standard oven without a special capability which is now available. Because each type of energy has advantages and deficits, most practitioners of New American Cuisine compromise and get both: gas for the cooktop stove and electricity for the oven.

Gas. In urban areas, gas is usually supplied by a municipal system; in rural locales, bottled gas is generally used. Professional gas contractors ensure that proper safeguards in plumbing and connection are employed in the system and that adequate pressure and regulation are provided. When planning your kitchen, keep in mind that straight runs of pipe provide the best pressure, that gas pipes fare best installed away from electrical cables and hot water pipes, and that flexible metal-hose connections are important for convenience and safety; they enable you to move the stove away from the wall in order to clean behind it.

Electricity. For major equipment, small appliances, ventilation and lighting, several separate electrical circuits are required. The number of circuits you need depends on the size and quality of the electrical system you want as well as on electrical code requirements, which vary from one part of the country to the next. Installing the proper voltage in the kitchens of houses generally presents no problem. It does in urban lofts and apartments, where no cellar or crawl space exists to facilitate the laying of electric cables. In apartment kitchens, snaking cables through the ceiling or under the floor often involves tearing the ceiling or floor apart to reach the space above or below, a measure both complex and costly.

Although code requirements vary from one part of the country to the next, there are typical guidelines for installing separate electrical circuits. A separate 220-volt circuit is needed for each heavy duty electric appliance: range oven, cooktop, dryer and certain air conditioners. A normal 120-volt circuit is needed for each refrigerator, freezer, dishwasher, clothes washer, and smaller air conditioners. The average kitchen requires only two 20-amp circuits for small appliances—automatic ice makers, compact refrigerators, trash compactors,

pilotless electrical ignition gas ranges and the like. Another 15-amp circuit is used by lights, clock, exhaust fan, radio, television and so on.

Duplex outlets—either continuous plug-in strips or separate receptacles—are needed every 4 feet of counter space. Special sockets are available with red light indicators that signal when power is on, an elegant refinement. Naturally, duplex outlets should be installed as close as possible to the work spaces for small appliances for which they supply power.

Water. At each end of the cooking process—preparation and cleanup—fast-flowing clean water is essential. New water-related appliances make this provision slightly more complex than before. Separate lines and drainage systems are needed for automatic ice makers and chilled drinking-water taps.

Island kitchens create the most complex problems for plumbing, especially those in urban lofts and apartments lacking under-floor crawl space. Even the increasingly popular open-plan kitchen—in which the cook has visual access to the guests while working—requires water pipes installed beneath the floor. Pipe runs under floor surfaces often cost more than electrical runs. The least expensive alternative is to have all water pipes installed against a core wall, although that doesn't make other plumbing

amenities possible. Efficient kitchen planning, however, should take precedence over economical plumbing.

If you own a country house that is closed for the winter, consider designing the water system for easy drainage. Protecting pipes from freezing is a complex, costly process—and there are no guarantees. At least pipes installed against interior walls freeze less quickly than exterior-wall installations do.

Water heaters and softeners are more economical if located near their point of use. Water softeners offer a number of advantages: they prevent pipes from scaling; they keep sinks and basins cleaner; they produce higher lather from soap; and they give the water a pleasant feel to the touch. Softened water also requires less soap or detergent. However, water softening systems take up a considerable amount of space, they are costly to install, and the chemicals do have a detrimental effect on some people's health. In addition, they require a by-pass tap for drinking water, which should not pass through the softening system.

Ventilation. At a time when environmental pollution is a nationwide concern, there is much talk about "indoor pollution" in the kitchen. More than any other room in the house, the kitchen accrues concentrated buildups of odors, grease, moisture and heat. These pollutants must be controlled to a greater or lesser extent by a system of ventilation. The varying degrees of importance you

assign to each pollutant determines the kind of ventilation system you need.

When it comes to ventilation, cooks generally think about odors first. The mouth-watering aroma of cooking food wafting through the air is something to be savored and enjoyed, not to be squelched. The acrid stench of a burned dish, or the pungent scent of sour milk, is a whole other matter. Good ventilation is also requisite for eliminating odors (and dangers) from gas stoves, water heaters, even washers and dryers. When these appliances create unpleasant smells, having an efficient exhaust fan is a godsend.

Most practitioners of New American Cuisine want a fan primarily to extract heat from the kitchen. This is more than a matter of convenience and comfort; it helps maintain a balance of temperatures. Controlling heat in the kitchen has important implications for the rest of the house as well. Moisture and gas are carried on hot air and settle on the nearest cool surface—whether it be a kitchen counter, a dish waiting to be served, a glass-top coffee table or a living room window. Even if your house is fully air-conditioned, exhaust ventilation in the kitchen is a must.

Exhaust fans have a number of installation possibilities. You can locate them through a wall, above a stove or in a window. If you opt for a window exhaust— which is the least expensive to buy and the simplest to install—keep in mind that window panes, curtains and nearby decorations will collect moisture and grease on their way through the unit. Window fans tend to rattle unpleasantly, another deficit. Of all the methods of kitchen ventilation, they are the least efficent.

There are two types of overhead hoods for stoves: ducted and ductless. Ducted hoods are the most expensive and it is not always possible or desirable to run a duct to an outside wall through a kitchen cabinet, floor or ceiling. Hoods—whether ducted or ductless— are generally located 22–30 inches above the stove. Ideally, they should have both high and low speed extractor capabilities. If your stove is equipped with a built-in grill, barbecue or wok, each should have a hood of its own. When hoods are located above kitchen islands, the overhead ducting is difficult to cancel. Ask yourself if you must hide such a hood or if you can live with it exposed as a sculptural ornamentation.

Ductless hoods trap pollutants in charcoal filters, much like aquarium filters do, and like aquarium filters,

the charcoal must be regularly changed. Some new range models have extractor exhausts built into the top of the units; these are ducted from below. Others utilize ductless carbonizer elements. For optimal control of odors and heat, ductless hoods should be installed in combination with other exhaust fans.

Waste Disposal. Perhaps because cleaning up is the last step in the cooking process, eliminating waste is usually the final consideration in kitchen planning. Frequently—unless a sink has been fitted with a garbage disposal unit or a trash compactor has been ordered—waste disposal is simply neglected or ignored until the rest of the kitchen has been fully installed. That's why so many cooks find themselves tripping over their trashcans later on.

A trashcan or bin is a requisite part of any kitchen, but if you plan where it will go in advance, it can be conveniently hidden. The key is to look upon waste disposal as a separate kitchen system in its own right. Consider the places where garbage typically accumulates—the cutting board, the sink, the preparation counters, the dining table after meals. Viewing trash as if you were a country dweller with no garbage collection service is a helpful exercise.

Foodstuffs can be eliminated in the garbage disposal unit of the sink, provided you live in an area where the drainage system and plumbing code will allow you to have one. In some parts of the country, disposal units are mandatory; in others, they are prohibited. Check your local plumbing code to determine whether you can't or must have one.

Burnable items as well as glass or metal can be disposed of in the trash compactor. A compactor is a handy device to own. It cuts down the number of trips you have to make to the trashcans outside and it provides optimal environmental protection. It makes a significant contribution to kitchen efficiency and convenience. Compactors reduce garbage to one quarter of its original bulk, although each compacted load weighs a good deal more than loose trash. Some compactors are available with automatic deodorizers and slide-out drawers which make opening the units easy—even if your hands are full.

Garbage cans and waste baskets should be hidden beneath sinks or on pull-out or fold-out units installed in

The Ranch Breakfast

You don't need a ranch to serve a ranch breakfast, only a collection of hearty appetites. And, of course, a taste for ample quantities of well-seasoned food. A ranch breakfast is appropriate at any time of year, during any season, at any hour of the day. Be sure to have a generous pot of coffee on the fire, as well as plenty of Worcestershire Sauce, Tabasco, catsup and prepared steak sauce. All will be liberally used.

base cabinets. Cutting boards are available with holes similar to restaurant-counter drops through which cuttings are caught by a bin underneath. Breadcutting boards also come with open slats for removing fragments or crumbs. If your kitchen will double as your laundry room, the clothes hamper should be concealed as a built-in bin with push-in drop or chute as well.

Special Equipment. A well-designed kitchen has future equipment needs preplanned into it, for later additions that were not considered at the outset can spoil the clean-lined appearance you strive so hard—and invest so much money—to create. Telephones, intercom systems, radios, television sets, stereo speakers, cookbook shelves—if they are to be part of your kitchen someday—must all be planned for in advance if the aesthetic appeal of your kitchen is important to you.

Everything should be conveniently located away from water, steam and heat and near electrical outlets—even your cookbooks, which require reading light. If you want a bulletin board in your kitchen—for grocery lists, reminders, phone messages—determine where it should go now, rather than hunting for a space to fit it in later on.

Paying careful attention to kitchen detail is in part an introduction to the experience of New American Cuisine. For all the decisions you make—about layout, materials, appliances, the varying functions your kitchen will serve—produce an environment that invites participation in every phase of the cooking and entertaining process. Your decisions collectively produce an atmosphere not just of functional utility but of visual delight as well. They become a personal statement—of who you are, what you like, how you live. To achieve that, it is well worth the time, effort and money you invest in planning your kitchen. It is that deep-rooted pleasure in the good things of life that makes living itself richer, more worthwhile, more meaningful, more fun. If New American Cuisine is about anything at all—it is about that.

A Ranch Breakfast
4. *Roast Beef Hash (p. 89)*
9. *Baked Apples (p. 142)*
10. *Tomato Pudding (p. 121)*
11. *Hashed Potatoes with Onions and Peppers (p. 129)*
12. *Pepper Corn Bread (p. 42)*
14. *Steak and Eggs*
15. *Buttermilk Blueberry Pancakes (p. 139)*
16. *Jalapeno Pepper Relish (p. 85)*
17. *Tomato Marmalade (p. 85)*

For product information, please refer to Credit Listing starting on page 151.

Frying Pans, Sauté Pans and Griddles

For all their numbers, top-of-the-stove pots and pans have their specific jobs. Beginning with the simplest, the flat surface of griddles is for cooking eggs, pancakes, meats and fish. The handsome copperbound soapstone griddle (12) needs no fat for cooking. Neither does the rectangular one (11) with its stick-free SilverStone®finish. Oil will be necessary, however, for the wooden-handled steel griddle (14) or the commercial aluminum one (8).

Designed especially for meats is the grill pan (1) so popular in Europe. Its ridged bottom works just like a grill.

For quick browning or frying in small amounts of fat, the frying pan comes in a range of sizes and should be made of a material that conducts heat well. The classic cast-iron one (9) is excellent, as is aluminum. Stainless steel is a poor heat conductor so make sure it has a bottom heavily sandwiched with aluminum, as this one does (13). Enamelled cast iron (4) does not brown food as well but is suited to longer and slower cooking. The

ultimate is copper (3). Besides being beautiful, it is the best conductor of heat.

For fried chicken and other dishes that need to be browned and then cooked in their own fat for a longer time over a gentle heat, use a frying pan with a domed lid. These pans should be heavy and hold heat well, as cast-iron or aluminum utensils do. The rapid heat conduction of copper is not necessary here.

Finally we come to the sauté pans with low straight sides that quickly sauté foods in small amounts of fat over high heat, permitting the tossing and stirring of the foods as they are cooked. Deep-sided pans allow sauces to be added while browning takes place. Often optional, the cover is useful. Because of the need for high heat, copper is the first choice of materials.

Eggs

Because eggs are omnipresent, it is easy to take them for granted. But it is hard to imagine a more versatile food. They serve equally well as a main course for breakfast, lunch or dinner. They are easily transformed into an appetizer, entree or dessert. They can be cooked almost any way you like. You can boil them, poach them, fry them, scramble them or bake them. You can even eat them raw, as in steak tartare or a Caesar salad. They are eminently compatible with other foods. Combined with milk and sugar they form the base for a custard: *Crème Renversée* to the French; *Flan* to the Spanish; cup custard to every American child. Eggs are part of many reduced stocks that are the basis of *New American Cuisine* sauces: Hollandaise, Bearnaise and Gribiche among them. Drop a raw beaten egg into a boiling chicken or beef broth and you have what the Italians call *Straciatella,* the Chinese egg drop soup. Chop up a hard-boiled egg, mix it with minced onion, chives and mayonnaise, and you have a delectable sandwich filling or salad. (A Jewish version combines the chopped eggs and onions with chicken fat instead of mayonnaise, a

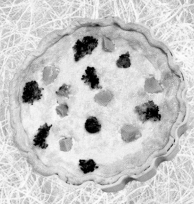
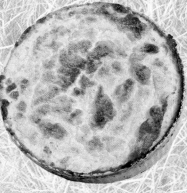

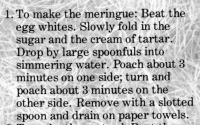

Ham and Broccoli Quiche
Pastry
5 tablespoons butter
5 tablespoons lard
2 cups flour
½ teaspoon salt
6-7 tablespoons ice cold water

Filling
3 eggs
1 egg yolk
1 tablespoon flour
pinch nutmeg
3 cups heavy cream
½ cup grated Swiss cheese
1 cup broccoli flowerets,
    parboiled
1 cup cubed ham

1. Prepare the pastry: Cut the butter and lard into the flour. Add the salt and ice water. Quickly shape into a firm dough. Chill for several hours.
2. Beat the eggs and combine the ingredients for the filling. Line a 10-inch pie plate with the rolled-out dough. Pour in the filling.
3. Bake in a preheated 375° oven for 35 minutes. Serve warm. Let it set for at least 10 minutes before cutting.

Cheese Soufflé
½ cup butter
½ cup flour
1 teaspoon salt
dash of freshly ground pepper
2 cups milk
2 cups shredded cheddar cheese
8 eggs, separated
¼ teaspoon cream of tartar

1. Melt the butter in a saucepan over moderate heat and stir in the flour and seasonings. Whisk in the milk, mixing thoroughly to avoid lumps, and cook over very low heat until mixture is thick and smooth.
2. Stir in cheese until it melts. Remove from heat and cool slightly (about 5 minutes). Beat egg yolks and add to the sauce, stirring constantly.
3. Beat egg whites with the cream of tartar until they are stiff but not dry—they should form peaks. Gently fold the cheese sauce into the egg whites. Pour into a buttered 2½-quart soufflé dish.
4. Run the tip of a knife around the dish about an inch from the edge—this makes it rise attractively. Bake in a 475° oven for 10 minutes, then lower heat and cook at 400° for 45 minutes or until browned and firm.

Oeufs en Gelée
2 packages unflavored gelatin
1 cup white wine
1 can concentrated beef
    consommé
2 tablespoons brandy or Madeira
    (optional)
1 tablespoon lemon juice
1 teaspoon salt

1. Dissolve the gelatin in the wine and heat gently. Add the remaining ingredients except for the eggs.
2. Cool the liquid, and pour about an inch into 4 molds or glasses. Refrigerate until set.
3. Drop a soft-boiled egg into the mold. Pour the remaining liquid over the eggs. Chill until set, at least 3 hours.
4. To unmold, run the bottom of the receptacle under running hot water, then turn upside down. The classic garnish is a slice of rolled ham and a few spears of asparagus.

Floating Island
Meringues
4 egg whites
¾ cup sugar
pinch cream of tartar

Custard
4 egg yolks
½ cup sugar
2 cups half-and-half

1. To make the meringue: Beat the egg whites. Slowly fold in the sugar and the cream of tartar. Drop by large spoonfuls into simmering water. Poach about 3 minutes on one side; turn and poach about 3 minutes on the other side. Remove with a slotted spoon and drain on paper towels.
2. To make the custard: Beat the eggs, sugar, and half-and-half together until well blended. Heat in a double boiler or over a low flame, stirring constantly, until the mixture coats the spoon.
3. Pour the custard into a bowl and float the meringue balls on top. Chill for several hours. The meringue balls can be decorated with slivers of chocolate or a dusting of cinnamon.

Gougère (Cheese Puffs)
1 cup water
1 stick butter
½ teaspoon salt
1¼ cups flour
¾ cup Swiss cheese, grated
4 eggs

tasty variation.) In addition to all this, eggs are high in protein, reasonable in calories, fairly low in cost.

Here are some tips for cooking with eggs:

When poaching eggs, add a spoonful of vinegar or lemon juice to the boiling water. It keeps the whites from dispersing.

When hard- or soft-boiling eggs, add a spoonful of vinegar to the water. Then, if an egg should crack, the white will not run out.

To find out if an egg is too old to use, set it in a bowl of water. If it floats, throw it out.

1. Heat water, butter and salt in a saucepan.
2. When butter is melted, remove from heat and dump in flour. Stir vigorously with a wooden spoon until mixture forms a ball.
3. Add the eggs, one at a time, beating hard, until each egg is completely absorbed. Mix in the cheese.
4. Drop mixture by large spoonfuls in a circle on a greased and floured cookie sheet. Bake in a preheated 450° oven for 10 minutes, then lower heat to 325° and bake 15 minutes more.

Western Omelet
2 tablespoons oil
2 tablespoons onion, chopped
¼ cup green pepper, coarsely chopped
¼ cup tomato, coarsely chopped
2 tablespoons ham, chopped
2–3 large eggs
pinch salt
2 tablespoons water
2 tablespoons butter

1. Make the omelet filling by heating the oil in a frying pan and adding the onion. Cook until golden, then add the green pepper and tomato and ham, and cook on a low flame for 3–4 minutes.
2. Make the omelet by beating the eggs with the salt and the water. Melt the butter in a non-stick or well-seasoned omelet pan. Add the eggs. Beat until just beginning to thicken, then allow to set.

3. While omelet is still soft and runny, pour the filling onto one side of it. Turn off the heat and let set for a few seconds. Then fold over half the omelet to cover the other half. Gently shake the pan to loosen omelet and slide onto serving plate. Omelet can be kept warm in a very low oven while other omelets are cooking. To make additional omelets, multiply the filling by the number of other omelets to be made.

Meringues
6 egg whites
1½ cups confectioner's sugar
pinch cream of tartar

1. Beat the egg whites with the cream of tartar. When just beginning to stiffen, add the sugar little by little. Beat until stiff and glossy.
2. Grease and flour a baking sheet. Form the meringues with a pastry bag into round or oval shapes. Or, lacking a pastry bag, they can be shaped with a large spoon.
3. Bake in a 200° oven for about 3 hours. If the oven gets too hot, leave the door ajar. The meringues will be off-white. Remove with a spatula from the baking sheet and store in a dry spot. May be served as is, as an accompaniment to fruit, or covered with whipped cream.

Crème Caramel
2 cups milk or half-and-half
1 cup sugar
½ vanilla bean or 1 teaspoon vanilla extract
4 egg yolks
2 eggs
½ cup water

1. Heat the milk and ½ cup sugar with the vanilla bean to almost boiling. Remove from the flame and cool 5 minutes. Whisk in the egg yolks and the whole eggs and beat thoroughly.
2. Heat remaining sugar and water on a high flame and cook until the syrup turns a light brown. Do not burn. Pour the syrup into baking dish and coat it well.
3. Pour the custard into the baking dish, set the dish in a pan of hot water and bake in a 400° oven for about 50 minutes. Test by slipping a knife into the center of the custard—if it comes out clean, the custard is done.
4. Cool the custard. It can be made ahead and refrigerated. To unmold, slip a sharp knife around the edge of the baking dish. Invert onto a serving plate, give a few shakes, and the custard should come out.

Egg Utensils

The versatile egg is the basis for a whole range of utensils. You'll need something to beat it, like the sturdy egg beater shown here (3). But if you make a lot of soufflés or meringues, a copper bowl and balloon wisk are necessities to beat the whites. The chemical reaction of the whites against the copper produces a greater volume of fluffiness than you can get any other way. And for easy breakfast maneuvering, add an egg turner (2), a poacher (7), and a really good omelet pan. If you really want to pamper yourself, use an egg separator (6), and a little whisk (1) that will quickly beat that one egg so often needed in recipes.

The English Breakfast

The traditional English breakfast was not born in the dining room but the bedroom, where Early Morning Tea was delivered by a servant on a tray. This consisted of tea and nothing but. It gave one the strength to throw off the covers and perform the morning's ablutions in a cavernous, unheated room. After which the lady or gentleman of the house would repair downstairs and sit down to a sumptuous repast, also designed to insulate the body against the onslaught of cold and damp. Today the English breakfast is what we typically call "brunch," an early lunch that is perfect for skiing, skating, joggers and other weekend sports enthusiasts, and Sunday noon entertainers who prefer the serve-yourself informality of a buffet.

An English Breakfast
1. Kidney Stew (p. 89)
2. Grilled Tomatoes and
Mushrooms (p. 123) Sausages
3. Porridge
4. Kippers (p. 111)
5. Kedgeree (p. 111)
8. Scrambled Eggs Canadian
Bacon
10. Strawberries with Clotted
Cream (p. 142)
12. Bran Muffins

Bread

Fresh, wholesome, satisfying bread has been the staff of life since biblical times. The recent demand for lighter, richer, more interesting breads has produced a spate of bakeries specializing in nothing but bread. It is now possible to buy a loaf or a croissant here in America that would do any Frenchman proud. While the making of bread, especially yeast bread, was once a time-consuming, laborious chore, it no longer need be. If you have a food processor or automatic mixing machine with a dough hook attachment, preparing even yeast dough has become as quick and effortless as making mashed potatoes or whipped cream. You don't have to use it all at once. Fix a big batch and store some of it in your freezer for baking at a later time. If you're short on time, there are a host of quick breads and muffins you can make. They can be mixed and baked while the rest of the meal is cooking. And piping hot bread straight from the oven is a welcome addition to any meal.

Easy Italian Bread
2 cups lukewarm water
1 tablespoon olive oil
1 tablespoon sugar
1 tablespoon salt
2 packages dry yeast
1 tablespoon oregano
5½-6 cups all-purpose flour

1. Dissolve yeast in the lukewarm water. Stir in the olive oil, sugar, salt and oregano. Gradually stir in the flour. The dough should be medium-stiff.
2. Turn the dough onto a floured board and knead for about 5 minutes. Add more flour if mixture sticks.
3. Place in greased pan, cover and let rise until doubled in bulk. Punch down and divide into 3 long fat loaves. Place on a cookie sheet and cut slashes in the tops of the loaves.
4. Let rise again in a warm place until doubled in bulk. Brush the loaves with water and bake in a preheated 400° oven for about 40 minutes, or until bread sounds hollow when tapped.

Riviera Toast (not shown)
1 loaf uncut day-old white bread
1 cup butter melted
1 tablespoon each salt, pepper, paprika, and mixed herbs

1. Cut bread into thick 2″ slices. Cut each slice into thirds.
2. Place on cookie sheet and paint both sides with butter. Sprinkle both sides with seasonings.
3. Broil in hot oven until brown. Turn and brown other side.

Easy Brown Bread
1 package yeast
1¼ cups warm water
2 tablespoons vegetable oil
1 tablespoon sugar
1 tablespoon salt
1 cup unbleached white flour
2 cups whole wheat flour
¼ cup sesame seeds

1. Dissolve yeast in warm water. Add oil, sugar and salt.
2. Stir in flour, one cup at a time, stirring thoroughly between each cup. If too sticky, add a bit more flour, but not more than ½ cup more.
3. Knead until dough forms a smooth ball. Place in an oiled

bowl, cover and let rise until double in bulk (about 1 hour).
4. Punch the dough, then knead a bit more with enough flour to keep from sticking to hands. Form into a loaf. Put in greased loaf pan. Let rise until almost filling the pan. Sprinkle with sesame seeds.
5. Bake in a preheated 375° oven for 45–50 minutes or until golden brown.

Rye Bread
3 packages dry yeast
4 cups lukewarm water
1 teaspoon sugar
2 tablespoons salt
1 cup mashed potatoes
2 tablespoons caraway seeds
15 cups light rye flour

1. Dissolve yeast in water. Stir in sugar, salt mashed potatoes and caraway seeds.
2. Gradually add 12 cups of flour and stir until smooth. Let rise in a warm place, covered, until doubled in bulk.
3. Pour onto a floured board and knead in the rest of the flour. You might need to use more flour. Knead for 5 minutes. Form into 5 loaves. Place loaves on a floured baking sheet and let rise until doubled in bulk.
4. Brush top of loaves with cold water and bake in a 425° oven for 15 minutes. Reduce heat to 350° and bake 45 minutes longer, or until loaves sound hollow.

Swiss Potato Loaf

2 packages dry yeast
2 cups very watery mashed
  potatoes, heated to lukewarm
2 tablespoons shortening, bacon
  fat or chicken fat
2 tablespoons sugar
1 tablespoons salt
6-6½ cups all-purpose sifted
  flour

1. Dissolve the yeast in the
   mashed potatoes.
2. Add shortening, sugar, and
   salt. Gradually stir in the flour.
3. Knead on a floured board until
   very elastic, about 5 minutes.
4. Place in bowl, covered, and
   leave in a warm place until
   doubled in bulk. Punch down
   and place in a large, round-
   greased pan. Cover and let rise
   again until doubled in bulk.
5. Bake in a preheated 375° oven
   for 45 minutes, or until bread no
   longer sticks to sides of pan. If
   the loaf pan is high and deep,
   rather than shallow, the bread
   will need to bake for about 1¼
   hours.

Pepper Corn Bread

1¼ cups milk
2 eggs, beaten
¼ cup bacon fat or oil
¾ cup flour
2½ teaspoons baking powder
¼ cup chopped jalapeño peppers
1½ cups yellow corn meal

1. Beat milk, eggs, oil, sugar, and
   baking powder together. Stir in
   jalapeño peppers, corn meal and
   flour, mixing well. Pour into a
   greased shallow pan. Bake for 25
   minutes in a 400° oven.

Challah

1 package dry yeast
2 teaspoons sugar
1¼ cups lukewarm water
2 eggs, beaten
2 teaspoons salt
2 tablespoons vegetable oil
4½ cups all-purpose flour, sifted
1 egg yolk, beaten
4 tablespoons poppy seeds

1. Combine yeast, sugar and ¼ cup
   lukewarm water.
2. When yeast is dissolved add
   eggs, the remaining 1 cup of
   water, salt and oil. Stir in the
   flour and knead on a floured
   board until smooth (about 5
   minutes).
3. Place in a greased bowl, cover
   and let rise in a warm place until
   doubled in bulk. Punch down,
   cover, and let rise again.
4. Divide the dough into 3 equal
   parts and roll into strips. Braid
   the strips together, sealing
   them well at both ends. Place on
   a baking sheet and let rise for a
   third time. Brush the top of the
   loaf with the beaten egg yolk
   and sprinkle with the poppy
   seeds. Bake in a preheated
   350°oven until golden brown,
   about 50 minutes.

Sourdough French Bread

2 cups warm water
1 cup sourdough starter (see
  Note) at room temperature
7½-8 cups all-purpose flour
2 teaspoons sugar
1 teaspoon salt

1. Combine warm water, starter,
   and 4 cups of flour in a bowl.
   Leave in a warm place, covered,
   for about 6 hours. Mixture
   should look bubbly and puffy.
2. Stir in salt, sugar and about 3
   cups of flour. The dough should
   be stiff.
3. Knead on a floured board until
   smooth, about 10 minutes. Add
   more flour if necessary to
   prevent sticking.

express yourself...

kathryn conover

How
to
turn
Charlie
Cologne

into
Charlie
Perfume.

Spray it on,
it's Charlie Cologne.
But hours later,
rub gently to release
the richer scent
of Charlie Perfume.

Charlie Perfume-in-Cologne.
The fragrance that awakens to your touch.
From Revlon.

4. Place in a greased bowl, cover and leave in a warm place until doubled in bulk. Punch down and divide into 2 long loaves. Place on a cookie sheet or in French bread pans.
5. Cut diagonal slits in the loaves, cover and let rise agian. Bake in a 400° oven for 30 minutes, or until bread sounds hollow when tapped.

Note: Sourdough starter can be found in speciality stores. For a more authentic touch, sprinkle the bottoms of the loaves with cornmeal. Just before baking, brush the tops with 1 teaspoon cornstarch which has been dissolved in ½ cup water.

Pumpernickel Bread

2 packages dry yeast
2 cups lukewarm water
½ cup cornmeal
6 tablespoons vegetable oil
¾ cup molasses
1 cup mashed potatoes
3 cups rye flour
1 cup whole wheat flour
3 cups all-purpose flour

1. Dissolve the yeast in the water. Stir in cornmeal, oil, molasses and potatoes. Mix thoroughly. Gradually add the flours. The dough should be rather stiff.
2. Turn onto a floured board and knead for 10-15 minutes, or until smooth and elastic. Add more all-purpose flour as needed.
3. Place dough in a greased bowl, cover and let rise until doubled in bulk. Punch down and form into 3 round loaves. Place on a baking sheet and let rise again until nearly doubled in bulk. Bake in a preheated 375° oven for 40 minutes, or until loaves sound hollow.

Note: For a darker loaf, add 2 tablespoons cocoa.

Irish Soda Bread

4 cups flour
½ cup sugar
1 teaspoon salt
2 teaspoons baking powder
1 teaspoon lemon juice
1½ teaspoons caraway seeds
1 cup raisins
1 egg
2 tablespoons vegetable oil
1½ cups buttermilk

1. Have all ingredients at room temperature. Combine flour, sugar, salt, baking powder and caraway seeds. Stir well. Add raisins. Beat the egg with oil, then stir in. Gradually add the buttermilk until you have a firm dough. It should be like a biscuit dough, not too stiff.
2. Place on a lightly floured board and knead for about 3 minutes until dough becomes smooth.
3. Flatten dough and place in a greased 9-inch cake pan. Cut a big cross in the center of the dough with a knife dipped in sugar. Bake in a preheated 375° oven for about 40 minutes or until a knife inserted in the center of loaf comes out clean.

Bran Muffins
2 eggs
¼ cup sugar
¼ cup molasses
1½ cups buttermilk
2½ tablespoons vegetable oil
1 teaspoon salt
1½ cups flour
1½ teaspoons baking soda
2½ cups bran

1. Beat eggs, sugar, molasses, buttermilk, oil and salt together. Add flour, baking soda and bran, stirring well.
2. Fill greased muffin pans and bake in a 400°oven for 25 minutes.

Buttermilk Biscuits
(about 25 biscuits)
2 cups flour, sifted
1 teaspoon salt
1½ teaspoons baking powder
½ teaspoon baking soda
1 cup buttermilk
4 tablespoons oil

1. Mix dry ingredients thoroughly together. Add buttermilk and oil and mix thoroughly. Knead lightly. Roll out onto floured board to ½-inch thickness.
2. Cut with biscuit cutter. Place on greased baking sheet and bake in 450° oven for 15 minutes.

Corn Bread Sticks
1½ cups yellow corn meal
¾ cups flour
2 tablespoons sugar
2½ teaspoons baking power
2 eggs, slightly beaten
1¼ cups milk
¼ cup melted shortening or oil

1. Sift dry ingredients together.
2. Add the eggs and milk. Mix thoroughly and pour into a greased corn bread pan or any shallow pan. Bake in a preheated 400° oven for 20–25 minutes.

Winter Lunch: Bread and Soup

It's simple. It's basic. It's honest. And yet an unfrivolous lunch of fresh-baked bread and steaming home-made soup on a frosty winter day conjures up an image appealing enough to make even the sated groan with pleasure. Prepare two or three hearty soups and no appetite will go wanting. Add a selection of breads, a tray of cheeses and a bowl of fruit. Who could resist?

A Winter Lunch
8. *Mediterranean Fish Soup (p. 50) with 14. Rouille (p. 85)*
10, 21. *Beef Minestrone (p. 51)*
12. *Easy Brown Bread (p. 48)*
13. *Cream of Chicken Soup (p. 47)*
16. *Challah (p. 42)*
17. *Irish Soda Bread (p. 43)*
18. *Easy Italian Bread (p. 41)*
19. *Japanese Soup: Yosenabe (p. 48)*
20. *Lentil Soup (p. 47)*

Cream of Chicken Soup
2 cups dry white wine
2 quarts water
1 boiling fowl
1 cup celery, chopped
1 cup onion, chopped
1 cup parsnips, chopped
1 cup carrots, chopped
1–2 parsley roots, chopped
2 bay leaves
⅛ teaspoon thyme
4 tablespoons flour
4 tablespoons butter or chicken
   fat
1 cup heavy cream
salt, freshly ground pepper and
   ground nutmeg to taste

1. Bring water to a boil. Add wine
   and fowl and cook for 1 hour.
2. Add celery, onionn parsnips,
   carrots, parsley roots, bay
   leaves, and thyme. Cook 1 hour
   more.
3. Remove fowl, cool and cut into
   bite-sized pieces.
4. In another saucepan, melt butter
   or chicken fat and stir in the
   flour. Add 1 quart of the chicken
   stock and stir well to prevent
   lumps. Add the cream, the
   chicken pieces, and the cooked
   vegetables. Add more stock if
   desired. Add salt, pepper and
   nutmeg.

Leek And Potato Soup
6 leeks, white parts only,
   well-washed and sliced
2 small onions, sliced
4 cups rich chicken broth
5 potatoes, peeled and sliced
2 cups milk
1 cup heavy cream
salt and freshly ground pepper

1. Cook the leeks and onions in the
   butter until wilted. Add the
   potatoes and chicken broth and
   cook over a low flame 30 minutes.
2. Pour in the milk. Pass through a
   vegetable mill. (A blender will
   not work for this soup because
   the leeks are stringy.) Add the
   heavy cream, stir to mix well and
   taste for seasonings. Chill.

Quick and Beautiful Borscht
2 cans sliced beets with juice
3 cups beef broth
juice of 1 lemon
1 medium onion, chopped
salt to taste
1 cup sour cream
fresh dill, finely chopped

1. Combine the beets, broth, lemon
   juice, onion and salt in a blender
   until smooth. Fold in sour cream
   and blend again.
2. Serve sprinkled with fresh dill
   or with a hard boiled egg,
   scallion and sour cream garnish.

Lentil Soup
¼ cup vegetable oil or chicken fat
½ cup onion, coarsely chopped
4 garlic cloves, peeled and
   chopped
½ cup carrot, coarsely chopped
½ cup celery, peeled and
   chopped
½ cup Italian flat-leafed parsley,
   chopped
3 quarts rich chicken stock
1 pound lentils
salt and freshly ground pepper to
   taste

1. Heat the oil or chicken fat and add
   the vegetables. Cook until wilted.
2. Add chicken stock and lentils and
   bring to a boil. Skim, lower heat,
   and simmer 2 hours or until
   lentils are soft.
3. Taste and correct seasonings.

Pumpkin Stew

½ cup oil
3 onions, chopped
4 garlic cloves, minced
4 cups pumpkin, cubed
2 green peppers, cubed
2 red peppers, cubed
4 ripe tomatoes, cubed
1 cup corn
2 tablespoons cumin seed
2 cups vegetable or beef stock
3 cups cooked brown rice
¾ cup raisins plumped in water
¾ cup roasted cashews
salt and freshly ground pepper to taste

1. In a large saucepan heat oil and sauté onion and garlic until wilted. Add pumpkin, peppers, tomatoes, and corn. Toss vegetables in pan with heat high until slightly cooked (about 5 minutes).
2. Sprinkle on cumin seed and add stock. Cover and simmer over low heat for about 20 minutes or until pumpkin is soft. If too much liquid has accumulated, remove cover and turn heat high until almost no liquid remains.
3. Fold in the brown rice and heat through. Fold in the raisins and cashews. Taste for seasonings.

Note: If pumpkin is unavailable, use a hard winter squash such as acorn or butternut.

Beef Minestrone

4 garlic cloves, peeled and smashed
4 tablespoons olive oil
1 pound stewing beef, cut into 1-inch cubes
3 medium onions, chopped
2 stalks celery, chopped
2 carrots, peeled and chopped
3 quarts water
1 cup Italian flat-leafed parsley, coarsely chopped
½ teaspoon oregano
1 large (32 ounces) can peeled tomatoes with juice
1 cup elbow macaroni
1 large can cannellini white beans
1 large can chick peas
1 package frozen peas
2 medium zucchini, chopped
½ pound fresh spinach leaves, shredded
2 red bell peppers or 2 pimentos, cut into small strips
salt and freshly ground pepper to taste

1. Brown the garlic in the olive oil and remove.
2. Brown the cubes of beef and remove.
3. Cook the onions, celery and carrots until wilted but not brown.
4. Add the beef, water, parsley, oregano, tomatoes and elbow macaroni. Cook for 30 minutes.
5. Add the remaining ingredients. Stir well and taste for seasoning, adding salt, pepper and more oregano as desired. Cook 15 minutes longer.
Serve with Italian bread and grated Parmesan or Romano cheese.

Sherried Tomato Bisque with Riviera Toast (next spread)

3 tablespoons butter or chicken fat
1 large onion, chopped
3 tablespoons flour
2 large cans (28 ounces) peeled tomatoes or 8-10 large, vine-ripened tomatoes
2 cups rich chicken stock
½ cup dry sherry
salt and freshly ground pepper
cup heavy cream, whipped with ½ teaspoon salt.

Riviera Toast (see p. 41)

1. Melt chicken fat or butter. Add onion. Stir, then cover and simmer over low flame until onion is wilted, not brown (about 3 minutes).
2. Sprinkle with flour, then pour in tomatoes and chicken stock. Stir well to dissolve any lumps in the flour. Bring to a boil, then lower heat and simmer 30 minutes.
3. Pass through food mill or purée in blender.
4. Add sherry. Adjust seasoning to taste with salt and pepper.
5. Serve with a bowl of whipped cream.

Corn Chowder

½ pound lean salt pork
1 onion, chopped
4 cups corn kernels
1 quart milk
2 cups chicken stock
salt and freshly ground pepper to
   taste

1. Sauté the salt pork and when
   brown, add the onion and cook
   until wilted. Drain fat.

2. Add the rest of the ingredients
   and heat for 15 minutes. Do not
   boil.

Mediterranean Fish Soup

4 garlic cloves, peeled and
   smashed
¼ cup olive oil
1 cup onion, coarsely chopped
1 cup leeks, coarsely chopped

½ cup celery, chopped
½ cup green pepper, chopped
½ cup carrots, peeled and chopped
1 large (32 ounces) can peeled tomatoes with juice
1 teaspoon saffron threads
¼ cup flour
1 cup dry white wine
3 cups bottled clam juice
2 pounds boneless fish fillets, such as halibut, haddock, or tilefish (do not use an oily fish like mackerel or herring), cut into large cubes
½ pound small shrimp, peeled and deveined (optional)
1 pound mussels or clams, well-scrubbed (optional)
salt and freshly ground pepper

1. Brown the garlic in the olive oil. Remove and discard.
2. Stir in the onion, leeks; celery, green pepper and carrots. Cook until wilted.
3. Sprinkle with flour and stir well. Add saffron, wine, and clam juice. Cook briskly for 15 minutes.
4. Add the fish fillets, shrimp, mussels or clams. Cook 5 minutes more. Taste for seasonings.

Japanese Soup: Yosenabe
8 large dried Oriental mushrooms
8 cups Ichiban Dashi soup base (see Note)
2 chicken breasts, boned and cut into strips
8 large raw shrimp, peeled and deveined
8 large sea scallops
1 bean curd, cubed
1 bunch scallions, cut into 2-inch lengths
2 cups spinach leaves, shredded

Garnish (serve in 3 bowls)
2 cups Japanese white radish or white turnip, grated
1 cup scallions, chopped
½ cup orange-flavored vinegar

1. Add boiling water to mushrooms and let stand 30 minutes.
2. Just before serving, heat the Ichiban Dashi soup base. When boiling add the strips of chicken Cook 10 minutes.

3. Add the remaining ingredients and cook 3 minutes longer.
4. Serve on a hot plate surrounded by the 3 small bowls of garnish, which guests can combine and use as a dip for the soup ingredients.

Note: *Ichiban Dashi,* a Japanese soup base, is made by combining 8 cups water with 2 sheets of dried seaweed and ⅓ cup dried fish flakes. The water and seaweed are brought to a boil and cooked for 5 minutes, then the fish flakes are added and the soup is removed from the heat. If your neighborhood does not carry Japanese provisions, a beautiful and tasty soup base can be made by combining 1 quart chicken stock and 1 quart beef stock.

Stew and Soup Pots

Every kitchen needs at least one large pot: for stews, soups, pasta, ears of corn, boiled beef, or great quantities of anything. If you can only afford one, choose a size that can hold the largest amounts you think you might want to cook. Tall and narrow ones like 2, 3 and 5 are best for soups and stocks so that the flavors have farther to simmer up through the liquid. Because most of the cooking done in these pots will use a lot of liquid and low heat, they needn't be of the same high quality as a saucepan, but they should have a substantial bottom to prevent foods from sticking or burning. Copper is needed only for aesthetic reasons. Aluminum, cast iron or stainless steel are equally practical and far less costly. When long, slow cooking is out of the question because of time, a pressure cooker (4) speeds up the job.

Basic Utensils

Wooden spoons for stirring, serving and scraping are practical because they stay cool and do not scratch any special finish that might have been applied to the pot. Slotted wooden spoons can double as a whisk and are useful for sauces and gravies. For scraping the last bit of goodness out of a mixing bowl you will need a rubber spatula, perhaps in more than one size.

The staple of the kitchen is the metal—usually stainless steel—cook's set of spoons and forks. The slotted spoon allows draining of vegetables, the skimmer eases the removal of fats from stocks and soups. The ladle, spatula and pot fork are equally valuable. If sauce making is your forte, there is a porcelain sauce spoon that is taste-free and stays cool enough not to curdle a delicate blend.

55

Knives

Good knives are absolutely essential in any kitchen. They make any job faster and easier. The most practical knives for the average cook are those with blades of high-carbon stainless steel. Plain stainless is too tough to sharpen well, and plain carbon steel rusts and discolors easily, although many professional cooks feel their slightly finer edge is worth the trouble of keeping them clean.

The best knives have a tang (an extension of the blade) that reaches into the handle, preferably the entire length, and is fastened to the handle by rivets. The handle itself should be hardwood, a plastic/hardwood composition, or nonslippery plastic.

You can manage most culinary chores with three knives: a paring knife (21), a medium-sized chef's knife or slicer (13, 15, 16) and a utility knife (19, 20) but as you get more daring in the kitchen it's nice to add some of the specialty knives and other sizes that we show here.

High-quality knives, properly cared for, offer a long life of service. Never cut on any surface harder than the knife. Store them so that the edges are separated.

Sharpen them as you use them, the way every good chef does. Use a carborundum for basic sharpening and a sharpening steel (7) for final touchup.

Cubing and Julienning

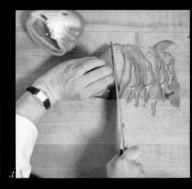

Cubing a carrot
1. Cut the carrot in half lengthwise so that it will lie flat on the board. The procedure is the same for most other vegetables as well.
2. Cut each of the two halves into two or three lengthwise pieces.
3. Hold the slices together at the thick end and dice into cubes.

Cubing Other Vegetables
1. Cut the vegetable into medium-thin julienne.
2. Assemble the julienne slices with your hands and slice vertically into cubes.

Julienning Vegetables
Julienning means to cut an ingredient into long, very thin strips. When potatoes are julienned for deep frying, they are called matchstick potatoes. Perhaps julienning is the most attractive of all the forms of cutting. Julienned vegetables make beautiful garnishes and salad ingredients.

1. Cut a thin slice from the vegetable so that it will lie flat on the cutting board.
2. Cut vegetable lengthwise into thin slices.
3. Stack three or four slices up and slice into thin matchstick slivers.

American Cookout

An aromatic wood or charcoal fire for grilling food, once a culinary necessity, has become a luxury. A sprawling barbecue, however, is not required. A simple hibachi will do quite nicely; it is one of the best types of grill on the market. Charcoal briquets make an excellent cooking fuel. Aromatic hickory chips, apple wood or old grape vine's (popular in Italy and France) will pleasingly scent the smoke and nurture the appetites of your guests. For extra aroma, add a handful of dried herbs to the hot coals: rosemary for lamb, sage for pork, marjoram or thyme for beef. All smell wonderful. Orange peels will produce a delicious smoky scent as well.

The most useful utensils include heavy asbestos gloves; tongs and spatula with long wooden handles; a good basting brush for applying marinades; a spotless hinged grill to hold the more delicate fish and meats; and skewers, either metal or wood, for brochettes. But remember to soak wooden skewers in water for a few hours before using them on a sizzling grill to keep them from charring.

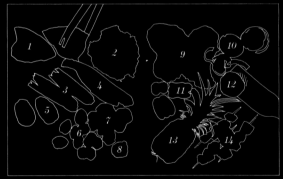

American Cookout
1. Swordfish (p. 111)
2. Mussels
3. Corn
4. Trout (p. 111, 113)
5. Potatoes (p. 129)
6. Clams (p. 113)
7. Oysters (p. 113)
8, 11. Bell Peppers
9. Butterflied Leg of Lamb (p.91)
10. Onions (p. 121)
12. Teriyaki Burger (p. 89)
13. Pineapple
14. Beef Brochettes

Hot Dogs and Cherry Tomatoes
Count on 1½ hot dogs per person and alternate on skewer with cherry tomatoes. Brush with oil. (not shown)

Eggplant and Whole Onion Skewers
Alternate chunks of eggplant, skin side out, with small, whole onions. Brush with oil while grilling. (not shown)

Skewers of Frankfurters and Mixed Vegetables
Alternate cubes of eggplant, zucchini, onion and frankfurters. Brush with oil, sprinkle with salt and pepper.

Skewers of Pineapple and Chicken
Count on ½ chicken breast per person. Cut skinned chicken into large cubes and alternate on skewer with a chunk of pineapple. Brush with ½ cup oil and ½ cup soy sauce while cooking. Can be marinated for several hours in this mixture.

Skewers of Beef, Peppers and Tomato
Alternate cubes of steak or ground beef balls with cubes of red or green bell pepper and tomato slices. Brush with oil while grilling.

Grilling Brochettes

These attractive and colorful skewers are easy to assemble and grill. Your imagination and taste will dictate combinations of fish, meat, vegetables and fruit. Skewers can be of metal or wood—soak the wooden ones for several hours in water beforehand to prevent burning. Following is a list of brochettes that you can make and a suitable marinade for each.

Scallop Skewers
Alternate scallops with reconstituted seaweed and cherry tomatoes. Brush with Terriyaki sauce while grilling.

Ham Chunks with Peppers
Make skewers of chunks of ham, red and green bell peppers (4 big chunks of ham per person). Brush with a sauce made of ½ cup oil, ½ cup soy sauce, 2 tablespoons Dijon-type mustard.

Skewers of Mushrooms and Bacon
Cut mushroom stems off at base, wrap each mushroom in bacon, and grill. No marinade is necessary—bacon is self-basting.

Brochettes of Shrimp
Count on 4 large shrimp and ½ red and ½ green bell pepper per person. Alternate shrimp and peppers on skewer. Marinate in 1 cup oil, combined in the blender with 2 garlic cloves, 2 teaspoons oregano, and red hot pepper flakes to taste.

Salads

Salads are the area of cooking in which it is easiest to give your imagination free play. The possibilities are endless and new combinations are being discovered all the time. The classic green salad is never out of place, no matter what else you serve. But feel perfectly free to vary the greens, oils, vinegars and herbs for refreshing changes of taste. Almost any combination of greens, cold pasta or rice, cold meats or fish, cheeses and raw or

Salad Nicoise

1 pound string beans, topped and cooked for 5 minutes in boiling salted water
3 medium-sized new potatoes, cooked and peeled & cut into bite-sized pieces
1 can of tuna fish
½ cup pitted black olives
1 small can of anchovy fillets, drained
1 head garlic, smashed with the side of the knife
½ cup finely chopped onion

6 tablespoons olive oil
2 tablespoons wine vinegar
1 teaspoon Dijon-type mustard
3 large ripe tomatoes, quartered
1 head romaine lettuce, broken into bite-sized pieces
3 hard boiled eggs, quartered (optional)
salt and pepper to taste

1. Toss the string beans and the new potatoes with the chopped onion, the oil, vinegar, Dijon-type mustard, and salt and pepper to taste. Set aside
2. Rub your serving bowl with the garlic, and discard clove. Arrange a layer of lettuce on the bowl or plate. Place the potatoes and string beans in their marinade on top of the lettuce. Place the tuna fish in the center, and garnish with the olives, anchovy fillets, tomatoes and eggs.

Oriental Sweet and Sour Salad

½ pound snow peas, topped and tailed
1 pound bean sprouts
1 green Bell pepper, cut into a fine julienne
1 red Bell pepper, cut into a fine julienne
1 tablespoon fresh ginger root, finely chopped
3 tablespoons oil (use Sesame oil for a spicier flavor)
4 tablespoons sugar
½ teaspoon salt
2 tablespoons soy sauce
3 tablespoons vinegar

1. Blanch snow peas in boiling water for 1 minute. Drain.
2. Combine snow peas, bean sprouts and Bell pepper slices.
3. Combine the ingredients for the sauce: the ginger root, oil, sugar, salt, soy sauce and vinegar. Pour over vegetables and toss well.
4. Refrigerate for several hours.

barely blanched vegetables can be assembled and artfully dressed to produce an attractive, light, satisfying lunch or dinner. Salads make an especially appropriate main course on a hot summer's day.

Mushroom Salad

1 pound very large, white mushrooms
2 lemons (juice)
1 cup chopped parsley
½ Bermuda onion, finely sliced (optional)
½ cup pimento, cut into julienne (garnish)
½ cup olive oil

1. Wipe mushrooms with a damp cloth and trim ends of stems.
2. Slice mushrooms into thin slices and toss with lemon juice, parsley and onion. Cover and refrigerate until ready to use.
3. Just before serving, toss with olive oil.

Note: If salt and pepper are necessary, add only at the last minute. Salt makes the mushroom slices watery

Spinach Salad with Bacon

1 pound spinach, well washed and dried and broken into bite-sized pieces (discard larger stems)
½ pound bacon, fried until crisp and crumbled coarsely
½ Bermuda (sweet) onion, sliced paper thin
1 large clove garlic, smashed
6 tablespoons oil
2 tablespoons wine vinegar
1 teaspoon Dijon-type mustard
salt and pepper to taste

1. Rub the salad bowl with the garlic clove and discard clove.
2. Combine oil, vinegar, mustard and salt and pepper.
3. Combine spinach in bowl with bacon and Bermuda onion. Pour over dressing and toss well.

69

Waldorf Salad

1 quart shredded escarole or
  other greens
6 Red Delicious apples, pared
  and diced
3 cups celery, peeled and diced
1 cup Walnut meats
2 carrots, shredded
1 cup raisins
1 lemon—juice

Dressing

3 tablespoons oil
1 tablespoon lemon juice
¼ cup heavy cream or sour
  cream
1 teaspoon sugar
salt and pepper to taste

1. Place pared and diced apples in
  a bowl and sprinkle with lemon
  juice to keep from darkening.
  Reserve 1 tablespoon lemon
  juice for dressing.
2. Combine apples, celery,
  carrots and raisins
3. Combine dressing ingredients.
4. Toss apple mixture with
  dressing and divide mixture
  evenly onto 6 chilled plates
  garnished with shredded
  greens.
5. Top with walnut meats and
  serve.

Mixed Vegetable Salad

¼ pound string beans, topped and
  tailed
1 medium-sized zucchini, sliced
1 carrot, cut into fine julienne or
  shredded
½ Bermuda onion, finely sliced
1 red Bell pepper, finely sliced
1 green Bell pepper, finely sliced
1 cup broccoli flowerets
1 cup cauliflower flowerets
6 tablespoons oil
2 tablespoons wine vinegar
1 teaspoon Dijon-type mustard
salt and pepper to taste

1. Parboil string beans for 3
  minutes; parboil zucchini for 1
  minute; parboil broccoli and
  cauliflower together for 1
  minute.
2. Toss vegetables together and,
  while cooked vegetables are
  still warm, dress with the oil,
  vinegar and mustard, and the
  salt and pepper to taste.

Caesar Salad

1 large head—approximately 2½ quarts—romaine or escarole, torn into small pieces
2 bunches watercress
½ cup grated Parmesan cheese
1½ cups freshly toasted croutons
3 tablespoons Worcestershire sauce
6 tablespoons olive oil
2 tablespoons wine vinegar
2 eggs, coddled for one minute and beaten together
1 small tin anchovy fillets, drained
1 large clove garlic, smashed with the side of the knife

1. Rub a large salad bowl with the smashed garlic clove. Discard clove.
2. Combine lettuce, watercress, Parmesan cheese, croutons and anchovy fillets. Set aside.
3. Combine Worcestershire sauce, oil, vinegar and the two eggs and beat well.
4. Pour dressing over salad, toss well and serve immediately.

Coleslaw

1 small head cabbage, finely shredded (about 4 cups)
2 carrots, shredded
4 scallions (green onions), thinly sliced
½ teaspoon salt
Freshly ground pepper to taste
5 tablespoons vegetable oil
2 tablespoons vinegar
1 teaspoon Dijon-type mustard

1. Combine oil, vinegar, salt, pepper, sugar and mustard.
2. Toss cabbage, carrots and scallions together to mix, and pour on dressing. Toss again, thoroughly, and refrigerate for several hours.

71

Cheese Utensils

There are as many kinds of knives and servers as there are kinds of cheese. Logically, you wouldn't expect the same knife that slices a hard cheese to cut a piece of runny brie. So there are planes, knives of several kinds, wedges and, for behind-the-scenes cutting of large pieces, double-handled knives and wires. For the basic kitchen, you'll need one cutter good for hard cheeses and one for soft.

To serve cheese the classic French way, use a willow tray. Or keep it cool in a terra cotta server, dipped in cold water first to keep the cheese at perfect serving temperature for hours. For easy storage, use a set of wooden cheese boxes.

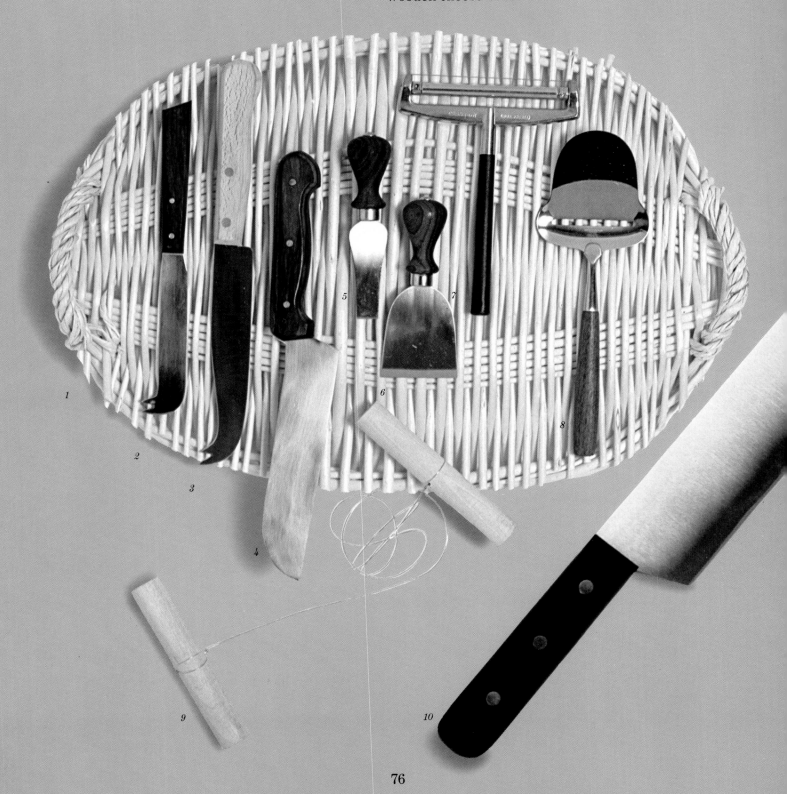

11

12

13

77

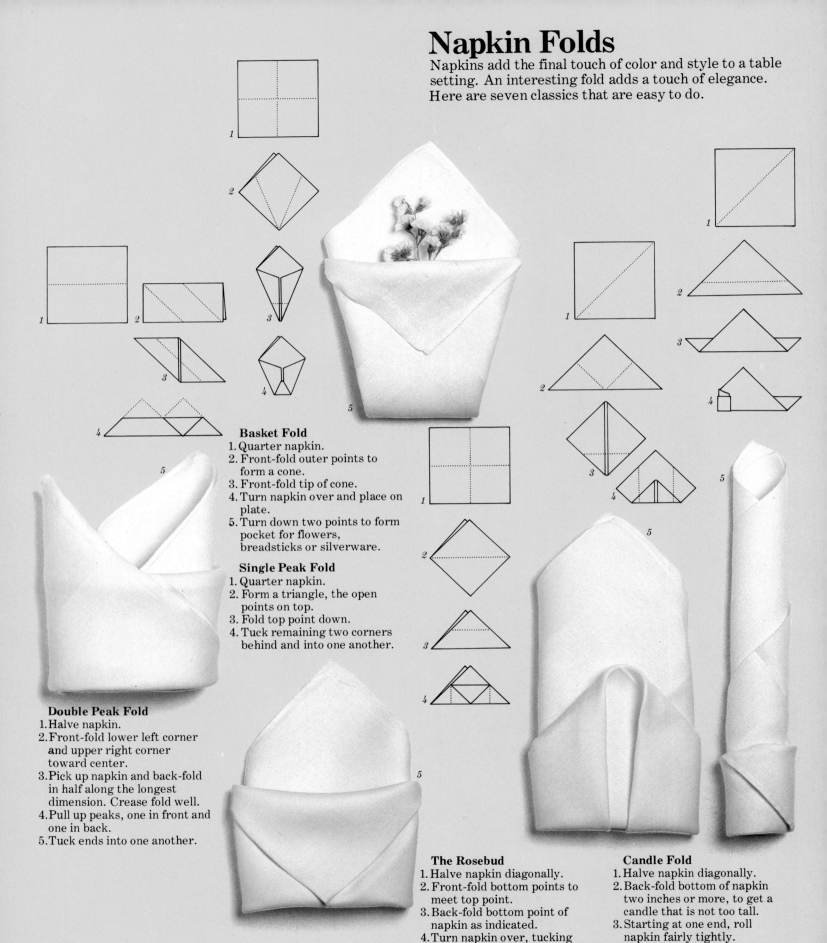

Napkin Folds

Napkins add the final touch of color and style to a table setting. An interesting fold adds a touch of elegance. Here are seven classics that are easy to do.

Basket Fold
1. Quarter napkin.
2. Front-fold outer points to form a cone.
3. Front-fold tip of cone.
4. Turn napkin over and place on plate.
5. Turn down two points to form pocket for flowers, breadsticks or silverware.

Single Peak Fold
1. Quarter napkin.
2. Form a triangle, the open points on top.
3. Fold top point down.
4. Tuck remaining two corners behind and into one another.

Double Peak Fold
1. Halve napkin.
2. Front-fold lower left corner and upper right corner toward center.
3. Pick up napkin and back-fold in half along the longest dimension. Crease fold well.
4. Pull up peaks, one in front and one in back.
5. Tuck ends into one another.

The Rosebud
1. Halve napkin diagonally.
2. Front-fold bottom points to meet top point.
3. Back-fold bottom point of napkin as indicated.
4. Turn napkin over, tucking side points into each other to form a stand.

Candle Fold
1. Halve napkin diagonally.
2. Back-fold bottom of napkin two inches or more, to get a candle that is not too tall.
3. Starting at one end, roll napkin fairly tightly.
4. Tuck remaining flap into bottom fold.

Fan Fold

1. Halve napkin.
2. Accordion-pleat three-quarters of the length, creasing well.
3. End folds so that all pleats are on the bottom.
4. With the unpleated section on your right, back-fold napkin in half with gathered pleats on the outside and pointing up.
5. Fold unpleated section diagonally and tuck into pleats to form a stand.
6. Set on plate and spread fan.

Scandia Fold

1. Halve napkin diagonally.
2. Front-fold two bottom points to meet top point.
3. Front-fold resulting bottom point to one inch below top point.
4. Reverse-fold bottom point down to meet bottom edge of napkin.
5. Back-fold, tucking sides into one another to form a circle.
6. Stand napkin up, adjusting two front points as shown.

Garden Party

A garden party can be a lunch. But more often it takes place between three or four o'clock on a summer afternoon, coinciding with the time of afternoon tea. And it is an afternoon tea appetite your guests will bring with them so they will probably not eat much. Nevertheless, the food should look fresh and summery and appear in abundance. Opulent array is a necessity here: The show's the thing. A balance of daintily feminine, heartily masculine, and a few highly sophisticated dishes ensures that you will have something for everyone.

A Garden Party

Sauce Pans are the most used pots in the kitchen, and you should buy the best ones you can afford. It's good to have several sizes, from small to large, to suit the job at hand, but if you will only have one, the three-quart size offers the most flexibility. Because copper is the best conductor of heat, copper pans have always been considered the best, but they require careful handling and the tin lining will need replacing from time to time—an expensive procedure. Copper pots with stainless steel linings (4) eliminate this problem, but are heavier and a little less efficient. Aluminum is second only to copper in

conducting heat, but you must be careful not to cook foods like eggs and tomatoes in them. The chemical reaction will cause the food to turn gray or the pots to pit. A process that permanently coats the aluminum has produced a new generation of aluminum pots that can be used for anything (2). Stainless steel, because it is less efficient in heat conduction, is generally sandwiched with aluminum on the bottom to improve the efficiency of the pot. Porcelain and enamel are particularly good for preparing eggs and tender sauces, where low heat and no interaction of metal are important. Because the

Double Boilers

water in the bottom will diffuse the heat, our beautiful hammered copper double boiler with a Limoges china insert is a luxury and no more efficient than the standard Pyrex glass pot. Look for double-duty features in these pots if space is a problem—a steamer insert for the same pot (14,15) or the second use of the pot as a saucepan. Another case of double duty: the enameled cast-iron pot whose top can double as a small frying pan (16).

12

14

13

16

15

17

Sauces and Gravies

Sauces in particular are a keynote of New American Cuisine. The glutenous flour and butter roux that has been used as a thickener for centuries is no longer in vogue, and that is just as well, for the heavy rich sauces of classical French cooking frequently overwhelmed and disguised the dishes over which they were served. Today's sauces are enriched and intensified by slowly reducing the stock to its essence. Thinner and clearer than classic sauces, they are designed to enhance rather than overwhelm, and as such they are often served *under* a portion of meat or fish rather than spooned on top. Yet these sauces and gravies are every bit as versatile as their forebears. They can play an integral part in the preparation of a given recipe or be served in a boat alongside the main course to provide a final flourish at the discretion of your guests. A sauce, however, need not be confined to a supporting role for the entrées you

Horseradish Sour Cream Sauce
1 cup (½ pint) sour cream
½ cup horseradish, freshly
   grated

Combine above ingredients.

Mustard Sauce (not shown)
1 cup heavy cream
½ cup Dijon-type mustard
salt and freshly ground pepper

Combine ingredients. Heat but
do not boil.

Green Tomato Pickle
(about 8 quarts)

8 quarts green tomatoes, sliced
½ cup salt
1 quart vinegar
1 cup sugar
2 tablespoons pickling spice
½ cup fresh ginger root,
   julienned
1 tablespoon dry mustard
1 tablespoon celery seed
1 tablespoon allspice, ground

1. Sprinkle salt over tomatoes and
   let stand overnight. Drain.
2. The next day combine tomatoes
   with remaining ingredients.
   Simmer for 20 minutes.
3. Pack into sterilized jars.

Mushroom Gravy (about 5 cups)
Neck, giblets of turkey
1 quart rich chicken stock
½ lb. mushrooms, cleaned and
   quartered
2 large onions, finely chopped
4 tablespoons butter, melted
4 tablespoons flour
½ cup Madeira (optional)

1. Add turkey neck and giblets to
   chicken stock. Bring to a boil and
   simmer, covered, for 1½ hours.
2. Sauté mushrooms and onions in
   butter over medium high heat.
   Sprinkle with flour and stir in
   stock. Simmer over a low flame
   for 30 minutes. Adjust
   seasonings and add Madeira.
   Add cooked chopped gizzard,
   heart and liver of turkey if
   desired.

Roast Beef Gravy (not shown)
4 tablespoons fat from roasting
   pan
4 tablespoons flour
2 cups beef stock
salt and freshly ground pepper to
   taste
1 tablespoon Madeira

1. Make a roux with the fat and the
   flour. Pour in the beef stock,
   whisking well to prevent lumps.
2. Cook 30 minutes on a low flame.
   Adjust seasonings and add
   Madeira.

Herb Sauce (not shown)
1 cup mayonnaise
1 tablespoon Dijon-type mustard
1 teaspoon each of rosemary,
   thyme, sage, and parsley,
   chopped

Combine ingredients. Serve cold.

Mint Sauce (not shown)
1 cup wine vinegar
¾ cup fresh mint leaves, finely
   chopped
1 tablespoon sugar

Combine ingredients and heat to
boiling.

make. It can be an elegant finishing touch for any course, from appetizer to dessert. While a sauce is rarely the star of the culinary show, it nevertheless often receives the most attention, a barometer for judging cooking skills. Culinary reputations are won and lost by the success of a sauce.

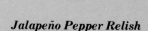

Cranberry Sauce
1 cup sugar
2 cups water
1 pound cranberries
1 orange peel, coarsely chopped

Boil sugar and water for 5 minutes. Add cranberries and boil until skins burst. Remove from heat. Cool. Stir in orange peel.

Sauce Rouille (not shown)
2 pimentos, chopped
4 garlic cloves
1 cup soft white bread crumbs, soaked in water and squeezed dry
2 hot chili peppers or Tabasco to taste
1 cup olive oil

1. With a mortar and pestle or in the container of blender or food processor, pound the pimento, garlic, breadcrumbs, and chili peppers. Make a thick paste.
2. Add olive oil very slowly, as if making a mayonnaise. Just before serving, stir in ¼ cup hot liquid from soup.

Sauce Gribiche
3 hard-boiled eggs, finely chopped

3 tablespoons wine vinegar
1 cup good olive or peanut oil
¼ cup mixed dill pickles, capers, parsley, finely chopped
¼ cup onion, chopped

Combine the ingredients. Chill and serve with fish.

Cumberland Sauce
1 cup currant jelly
1 orange, zest only
1 lemon, zest only
3 shallots, chopped
½ cup port wine
salt and freshly ground pepper

Combine the ingredients. Heat gently for 15 minutes. Serve at room temperature.

Dill-Mustard Sauce
(about 1½ cups)
½ cup Dijon-type mustard
1 tablespoon dry mustard
6 tablespoons sugar
⅔ cup peanut oil
4 tablespoons white vinegar

¼ cup fresh dill, finely chopped
salt to taste

1. Put Dijon mustard into a mixing bowl. Add dry mustard and sugar. Stir with a whisk to blend.
2. Gradually add oil, whisking constantly. Add vinegar, dill and salt.

Tomato Marmalade
(about 1 quart)
2 oranges, seeded
2 lemons, seeded
4 pounds ripe tomatoes, blanched, peeled, and drained
1 teaspoon cinnamon
1 teaspoon powdered cloves
¼ teaspoon powdered nutmeg
5 cups sugar

1. Peel the skins from the oranges and lemons and cut into thin strips. Do not use any white pith. Cut the oranges and lemons into chunks.
2. Combine all the ingredients in a large saucepan. Cook, uncovered, for about 1 hour, over a low flame. Tomato mixture should be thick. Skim off froth and pour into sterilized jars.

Curry Mayonnaise (not shown)
1 cup mayonnaise
1 tablespoon lemon juice
curry powder to taste

Stir all ingredients together.

Jalapeño Pepper Relish
(5–6 six-ounce jars)
¾ cup green Bell peppers, seeded and finely chopped
½ cup jalapeño peppers, finely chopped
1 cup vinegar
5 cups sugar
1 6-oz. bottle fruit pectin (Certo)

1. Combine Bell and jalapeño peppers, vinegar and sugar. Bring to a boil, lower heat and simmer 5 minutes. Skim surface. Remove from heat and stir in fruit pectin. Add red or green food coloring if desired.
2. Pour into hot, sterilized jars and seal.

Roasters

Roasters must be, above all, sturdy because they are used for big pieces of meat. This sturdiness and the size are more important than the material, since heat conduction or contact with acid foods is not a factor. Aluminum is light, sturdy, and economical and therefore a sensible choice. High or low sides, covered or open, are a matter of choice. You'll rarely use the cover except when you're roasting a turkey, but you might want to use the roaster as an oversized casserole.

Beef

We hear the term beef and automatically think of steaks and roasts. But beef encompasses a number of other cuts of meat as well, cuts that are used to produce dishes as diverse as Hungarian goulash, pot au feu or the sophisticated carpaccio of Italy. The various cuts are available in any of five grades ranging from a low of "utility" to a high of "prime." For steaks and roasts, choose the best quality beef you can find. It ensures that the meat will be tender and the flavor good. But for recipes calling for long, slow cooking, the grade of beef used is far less important. Prolonged exposure to heat will tenderize cuts that might otherwise be tough. Take the time to become familiar with the various grades and cuts available, and you will have no difficulty selecting the kind of beef appropriate for the recipe at hand.

Rib Roast of Beef

3-rib roast
salt and freshly ground pepper to
    taste

1. Place beef in a pan and rub with salt and pepper. Place fat side up. Place in preheated 500° oven 20 minutes.
2. Lower heat to 300° and continue cooking—16 minutes a pound for rare, 18–22 minutes a pound for medium-rare. A roast thermometer should read 140° for rare, 160° for medium.

Carpaccio with Dill-Mustard Sauce

A 3½–4-pound eye round, very
    lean
½ cup soy sauce
½ cup brandy
Tabasco

1. Marinate the eye round in soy sauce, brandy and a dash or two of Tabasco for 3 days. Turn every morning and evening in refrigerator. Do not marinate in an aluminum utensil.
2. Bring meat to room temperature. Preheat the oven to 500°. Roast the meat for 25 minutes, uncovered, in a lightly oiled pan. Reserve the marinade, which keeps almost indefinitely, for your next Carpaccio.
3. Remove the meat from the oven and chill overnight. When very cold (you may even want to chill it in the freezer for a few hours), slice paper-thin.

Stir-Fried Beef with Snow Peas
2 pounds flank steak
2 tablespoons cornstarch
¼ cup soy sauce
¼ cup cooking oil
1 pound snow peas, topped and tailed

1. Slice beef into thinnest possible slices. Discard any fat. Dissolve cornstarch in the soy sauce and toss beef pieces in this.

2. Heat oil in a wok or skillet. Toss in the snow peas and cook for a minute or two. Remove with a slotted spoon.
3. Heat oil to very hot and stir-fry beef slices for no more than a minute—they must remain very rare. Add snow peas, stir briefly, and serve.

Kidney Stew
6 beef kidneys, well trimmed, cut into bite-sized pieces, and soaked in milk overnight
4 tablespoons oil
4 tablespoons flour
2 cups beef stock
salt and freshly ground pepper to taste
1–2 tablespoons Madeira, (optional)

1. Dry the kidneys and sauté in hot oil. When well browned, sprinkle with flour and pour in the beef stock. Cover and simmer kidneys for 1 hour. Adjust seasonings and add Madeira. Serve in a chafing dish.

Roast Beef Hash
2 tablespoons bacon fat or oil
1 cup onion, coarsely chopped
4 cups cooked roast beef, cubed
1 cup cooked potato, cubed
1 cup beef broth
2 tablespoons Worcestershire sauce

1. Heat oil or fat in large skillet and add onions. Cook over low flame until wilted but not brown. Add remaining ingredients and cook, uncovered, over low flame for 45 minutes. Add more broth if necessary.

Teriyaki Burgers (not shown)
3 pounds ground beef

Teriyaki Sauce
1 cup soy sauce
½ cup sherry
2 teaspoons ground ginger
4 garlic cloves, pressed
oil

1. Combine the teriyaki sauce ingredients.
2. Combine the ground beef with ½ cup of the sauce. Mix well and shape into patties. Brush patties with oil. Broil burgers to desired degree of doneness, brushing every two minutes with oil. Serve with teriyaki sauce.

Veal

Of all meats, veal is the most delicate, and its subtle flavor makes it compatible with a variety of sauces and side dishes. The finest veal comes from a calf that is less than three months old. The meat is young and tender at that age, the flesh so pale that it is almost white. As veal continues to age, the flesh grows increasingly rosy and increasingly tough. If you use the color as your guide and choose the palest veal, you won't go wrong.

Veal Casino

1 pound salted butter
½ green pepper, diced
½ red pimento, diced
2 shallots, finely chopped
2 tablespoons parsley, chopped
4 tablespoons lemon juice
2 tablespoons Worcestershire sauce
freshly ground pepper
4 small veal scaloppine, cut from the leg

Casino Butter

3 tablespoons butter
2 tablespoons lemon juice

2 tablespoons flour
¾ cup beef broth
2 carrots, julienned

1. Make the Casino Butter ahead of time and store in the freezer. Roll it into a cylinder the breadth of a silver dollar and slice off as needed. It is excellent for vegetables, fish, steak, chops and potatoes.
2. For the veal: Heat the butter in a frying pan and sauté the veal very quickly on both sides. Sprinkle with lemon and remove. Stir in flour and broth, cooking for 3 minutes over a high flame. Pour over veal in serving dish and decorate with slices of Casino Butter and julienned carrots.

90

Lamb

Fresh American lamb most often makes a dinnertime appearance as a roast, as chops or in a stew. While all are superb, they are but an introduction to the many splendid ways this flavorful meat can be prepared. For a change of pace, try boning a leg, marinating it with herbs and grilling it whole, as we've done here. It's easy to do and your guests will love it. Or skewer chunks of lamb for a succulent shish kebab, as residents of the eastern Mediterranean do from Egypt to Greece. Lamb is a highly versatile meat. You can boil it, braise it, roast it, barbecue it or chop it up for cocktail meatballs or a savory moussaka. It serves equally well as a base for Moroccan couscous, Indian curry, Indonesian rijsatafel, French ragout or Irish stew. Browse through your cookbooks and you'll find dozens of tantalizing ways it can be served. A small word of caution: The flavor of lamb intensifies as the meat matures. Year-old lamb becomes mutton and has a strong, pungent taste. The English prefer it that way; you might not. Avoid aged lamb at dinner parties unless you are confident your guests will like it.

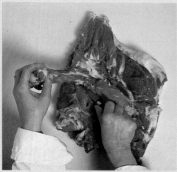

Butterflying a Leg of Lamb
1 leg of lamb
1 very sharp small knife
1 boning knife

The key to successfully boning a leg is to always keep your knives *very sharp*. Sharpen them frequently on a whetstone as you go along. Always keep the cutting edge of the knife turned in towards the bone.

There are three bones: the center leg bone, the shank bone, and the rump bone which is shaped like a small fist.

1. Turn the leg bone side up and run the knife along the rump bone. Work the blade around the bone to loosen it, keeping the blade close to the bone. The blade should be against the bone as you cut. Remove the rump bone and put it aside for soup stock.
2. Run the point of the blade close to the bone all the way to the end of the shank. Work the knife all around the bone until it is completely exposed. Remove this bone and reserve it with the others.
3. After the rump bone is removed, start cutting at the ball joint of the center leg bone. Make a straight cut at the center of the leg until the blade reaches the next joint, known as the stifle joint. Work the point of the blade around the stifle joint and all around the length of the center leg bone until the bone is completely exposed. Remove the bone and reserve it.
4. Spread the leg flat for broiling. When broiled for about 45 minutes, the thickest portion of the butterflied leg will be rare, the middle will be medium, and the edges will be well done.

(Courtesy of the American Lamb Council)

Butterflied Leg of Lamb
1 large leg of lamb
Marinade and Basting Sauce
2 cups peanut or vegetable oil
4 garlic cloves
1 tablespoon rosemary
2–3 dashes Tabasco
4 tablespoons Worcestershire sauce

1. Place ingredients for marinade and basting sauce in blender and blend until smooth.
2. Bone out the leg of lamb as shown or have the leg boned by your butcher. To keep the lamb from curling at the edges and to allow for more even cooking, place skewers inside the meat along the edges or place a hinged grill on top of your regular grill.
3. The lamb is best if marinated for one day on one side, one day on the other side. Place marinade in a shallow non-metal pan and refrigerate. Remove lamb from refrigerator about two hours before grilling.
4. Place the leg of lamb on the grill and brush every 10 minutes with the marinade. Cook the lamb about 20 minutes on one side, then turn and cook 20 minutes on the other side. Slice the meat thinly on the diagonal, as for a London Broil, and serve with one of the following sauces: mint, mustard or herb sauce (see p. 84)

Bowls and Things

Stainless steel bowls (7) are strong, lightweight and respond to heat and cold quickly. Ceramic bowls can be used in the oven. These (8) have a special flat side making them easier to hold while beating or mixing. Strainers for separating solids from liquids (6) and sieves for

pureeing (14) come in assorted sizes and with meshes ranging from fine to coarse. A colander (2) is used for draining pasta and other hot foods and for washing vegetables and fruits. If you can only have one, buy the biggest one that is practical for your space. But since you will need several sizes of bowls, strainers and the like, buy sets that nest into each other to save valuable shelf space.

Oven Pans

This selection of open pans used primarily for oven cooking ranges from a small porcelain dish in which to shirr an egg (15) to a large oval earthenware dish (22) that could hold potatoes au gratin for a crowd. Most are ovenproof glass, earthenware, enameled iron or porcelain, all materials that are perfect for the slow, gentle cooking of oven dishes. Those in copper and other metals can be used in the oven, but are really gratin pans to be slipped under the broiler for a finishing glaze and then brought to table. The exception: the traditional paella pan (3,4) where the rice and seafood, chicken, and sausage bake in the oven until done. If you're going to cook a soufflé, you'll need a straight, high-sided soufflé dish (11,14,25). Otherwise the size, shape and material will depend on your needs and taste. And if you'll generally be cooking for just a few people, consider letting one of the larger pans serve as your roaster as well.

30

16 *17* *18* *19*

20

22 *23*

21

24 *26* *27*

25

28

Casseroles

For the long, slow cooking that blends and mellows the flavors of meats and vegetables, a casserole is a necessity. The lid keeps the flavorful juices from escaping and lets the contents steam in their own broth, a function that is carried to its utmost in (6) whose top holds ice cubes to help condense the steam and return it to the dish, a traditional French technique. Again, ovenproof glass, earthenware, enameled iron, porcelain and low-heat-conduction metals like stainless steel are best. Some of these casseroles make the transition from oven to stove top easily (1,11,15,20), another way of saving space in the small kitchen. Others, like the pâté terrines (16,18) are designed with a specific use in mind. And the clay pot (10) is a modern version of the clay cooking methods used by the first cooks over an open fire. It has the plus of cooking quickly without grease or basting.

Pork and Ham

Fresh pork is a mildly flavored meat and should be seasoned well. Marinating the meat before cooking is often a good idea—it increases flavor and serves as a tenderizer. While it is important to cook pork thoroughly, it must not be done with such fervor that the meat becomes dry. If the juices have lost their pinkness and turned clear, if the meat itself no longer looks raw

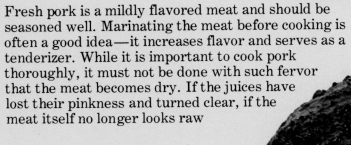

carefully without tearing fat. When ham is completely cold, trim off excess fat.

3. Sprinkle with freshly ground black pepper and coat with 1½–2 pounds brown sugar. Bake 45 minutes at 350°, basting frequently with apple cider or water. The outside of the ham should be a rich brown. When cool, carve with a long, sharp knife into the thinnest possible slices.

Country Pâté
2 pounds veal, cut from the leg
1 pound pork
1½ pounds ground pork
Marinade
½ cup brandy
¾ cup Madeira
1½ teaspoons salt
2 teaspoons freshly ground pepper
2 shallots, chopped
2 garlic cloves, peeled and smashed

1 teaspoon thyme
1 carrot, sliced
1 onion, sliced
½ teaspoon ground nutmeg
3 bay leaves
½ cup Italian flat leaved parsley, finely chopped

1. Cut veal and pork into julienne strips and place in a deep bowl. Mix marinade ingredients and pour over meat. Pat the ground meat into a flat layer and cover the julienned meat like a blanket. Cover bowl and refrigerate overnight.
2. The following day, remove the ground meat from the bowl. Discard carrot, onions, bay leaves, and garlic.
3. Line a loaf pan with bacon. Pat a layer of the ground meat into the pan. Alternate meat strips with ground meat, ending with a layer of ground meat. Pour on marinade liquid. Cover with remaining bacon. Place 3 or 4 bay leaves on top. Cover with foil.

Barbecued Spare Ribs
3 pounds spare ribs
½ cup soy sauce
2 tablespoons honey
2 tablespoons sherry
1 clove garlic, crushed

1. Place ribs in a shallow pan.
2. Mix remaining ingredients and pour over ribs. Roast in a slow oven for about 2 hours. Turning the ribs every 30 minutes.

Cooking and Baking A Smithfield Ham
1. Soak the ham in cold water to cover for 24 hours. Scrub the ham with a stiff brush to remove the mold and the pepper coating. Rinse.
2. Place the skin side down in a ham boiler. Cover completely with cold water. Two pounds of brown sugar can be added to the water for a sweeter taste. Bring to a boil, lower heat, and simmer 20 minutes per pound. A skewer stuck into the meaty part should come out easily. Remove ham from water and cool. When cool enough to handle, remove skin

and appears light gray, it is time to remove the pork from the oven.

Smoked and cured, pork is transformed into ham or bacon. The taste and texture of ham is governed by the cooking method used. All are delicious. But you need not buy an uncooked cut of meat. Fully cooked hams are readily available, and they can be a real timesaver. You don't have to soak or boil them. But even a precooked ham should be reheated before serving, and something extra—a simple glaze or a delicate wine sauce —provides an elegant finish.

The Holiday Dinner

The holiday dinner is a formal tradition. It does not call for gastronomic innovation. The roast turkey or goose, the homely accoutrements of turnips or brussel sprouts or mashed potatoes are important for preserving the nostalgia, for rekindling the memories of years gone by. That is why these meals have become traditions in the first place. But while the holiday dinner does remain more or less constant year after year, it is nevertheless given color and individuality by customs and traditions. It is the blend of ethnic flavor with the classic American holiday feast that makes it unique to your family.

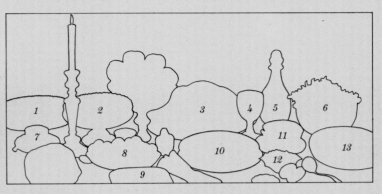

Holiday Dinner
1. Apple Pie, Cheddared (p. 139)
2. Pecan Pie (p. 139)
3. Roast Turkey (p. 102) Apple and Chestnut Stuffing (p. 102)
6. Green Salad
8. Brussels Sprouts with Chopped Almonds (p. 12)
9. Braised Onions (p. 121)
10. Sherried Tomato Bisque (p. 48)
11. Mushroom Gravy (p. 84)
12. Cranberry Sauce (p. 85)
13. Mashed Turnips and Potatoes (p. 128)

4. Bake in a pan of water in a 350° oven for 2 hours. Test for doneness by examining the fat on the surface of the pâté. Cloudy fat means the pâté is still exuding blood and is not yet done.
5. Weight the pâté by placing a can wrapped in foil on the top. This makes the pâté easier to cut when cool. Refrigerate overnight. Cut with a sharp knife while the pâté is in the pan.

Szechuan Twice-Cooked Pork
4 tablespoons hoisin sauce
2 tablespoons water
¼ cup oil
2-pound piece boneless pork, previously roasted, thinly sliced into strips.
1 garlic clove, finely chopped
1 bunch scallions, washed, trimmed and cut into 1″ pieces
4 slices fresh ginger, julienned
½ teaspoon tabasco

1. Combine hoisin sauce with water.
2. Heat oil in skillet and toss in pork. Add the remaining ingredients. Stir-fry for about 3 minutes.

Sunday Dinner in America

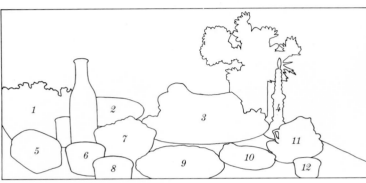

Fish

Fish has grown in popularity over the years as our knowledge of nutrition and cooking has increased. We have discovered that fish are healthy to eat—they are high in protein and low in fat. Fish taste delicious cooked any number of ways: poached, baked, broiled, stewed, pickled, or in a mousse. It is wonderful served raw as in the sushi and sashami favored by the Japanese. And a wider, more exciting variety of fresh fish is now available in local markets. When making a selection, keep in mind that white fish are more delicate in flavor and less oily in

Fresh, natural, basic, hearty food is the byword here. And simply prepared—that is the heritage left us by our colonial forebears. With the resurgence of interest in good health, the growing of gardens, and the eating of fresh, natural foods the *New American Cuisine* is perfectly suited to the Sunday dinner. It is the perfect harmony of old and new. The tradition, it seems, will endure. If you have visiting friends or relatives from another country, this is the meal of which they should surely partake: it is pure Americana.

Sunday Dinner In America
1. Mixed Green Salad
2. Pumpkin Chiffon Pie (p. 38)
3. Rib Roast Beef (p. 88)
Roasted Russet Potatoes
(p. 129)
5. Easy Brown Bread (p. 41)
6. Green Tomato Pickle (p. 84)
7. Stir-Fried Spinach and Cress
(p. 121)
8. Horseradish Sour Cream
Sauce (p. 84)
9. Corn Chowder (p. 50)
10. Cornbread Sticks (p. 44)
11. Roast Beef Gravy (p. 84)

Stuffed Bass with Sauce
Gribiche (p. 84)
1 cup breadcrumbs
½ cup parsley, chopped
½ cup onion, chopped
1 egg

salt and freshly ground pepper to
    taste
3–4 pound bass, boned

1. Combine breadcrumbs, parsley, onion, egg, salt and pepper. Stuff bass with this mixture.
2. Wrap fish firmly in well-oiled foil. Bake in a 350° oven for 40 minutes. Cool and remove foil.

texture than fish with darker meat, such as bluefish and tuna. There is one undeviating rule of thumb: the catch must be utterly fresh. If the fish in question is firm, if it smells fresh, if it is a whole fish with the eyes bright and clear, if the skin shines, if the gills are almost luminously red, you know it is a prize catch.

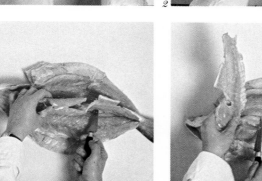

1 *2* *3*

4 *5*

6

Kippers
1 cup water
4 kippers, halved

Garnish
¼ cup parsley, chopped
1 lemon, quartered

Pour water into a large saucepan. Add the kippers, cover tightly, and steam for 15 minutes. Garnish with parsley and lemon.

Kedgeree
½ cup water
3 cups cooked rice
1 six-ounce can salmon, drained
2 hard-boiled eggs, coarsely chopped
¼ cup parsley, chopped

1. Bring the water to a boil in a saucepan and pour in the rest of the ingredients; cover and steam through.

Swordfish Steaks Véronique
(not shown)
8 swordfish steaks
oil for brushing on fish
8 small clusters green seedless grapes
8 small bunches curly parsley
4 lemons, halved

1. Brush swordfish steaks liberally with oil. Grill over hot coals approximately 5 minutes on each side. Baste frequently as fish tends to dry out.
2. Serve one swordfish steak to each person and garnish with a cluster of grapes, parsley and half a lemon.

Trout Wrapped in Bacon and Ham (not shown)
8 fresh trout, cleaned
8 slices best-quality smoked ham
8 slices bacon
salt and freshly ground pepper

1. Sprinkle the trout's cavity with salt and pepper. Wrap the trout in a slice of ham, then in a slice of bacon.
2. Place the trout on a folding grill and cook for approximately 5–7 minutes on each side. To test carefully flake exposed flesh of a fish—it should flake easily.

Boning a Fish
1 sea bass or striped bass, cleaned and scaled
1 very sharp small knife
1 boning knife
Any fish with a central backbone can be boned—salmon, sea trout, mackerel, herring, whiting.

1. With a small knife work around the bones that radiate out from the central backbone. Start at the head, near the gills, and work down to the tail. Snap or cut off the bone by the tail. Do this with both sides.
2. Work the backbone loose with your knife, or, in the case of a smaller fish, simply run your fingers down the backbone, "unzipping" it, from the flesh.
3. Go over the boned inside of the fish carefully and pick out any remaining bones. Slice off the fins.
4. Rinse off the fish and pat dry. Fish is now ready for stuffing.

Note: When boning oily fish such as mackerel, herring and salmon, keep half a lemon or a glass of vinegar handy. Constantly dip fingers into this to remove oily smell.

Fish Utensils

If you're a fish lover, you may want one or more of these fish-oriented utensils. They are specially designed to help clean and prepare your fish and seafood and are the ideal pots to poach (2), grill (3), or steam (4) them to perfection.

Clay pots can cook meat and poultry as well as fish, but the clay tends to absorb some flavor. Therefore it is best to keep this specially designed long and narrow cooker for fish only (1).

Shellfish

Lobster, crab, squid, shrimp, snails, clams, oysters and mussels are made to order for easy preparation. Shellfish is elegant to serve, delicious to eat, as high in protein and as low in fat as bony fish but with twice the mineral content. And shellfish is eminently adaptable. There are a variety of mouthwatering ways to serve shellfish— from the elegant simplicity of a plate of raw oysters on ice, to the pure refinement of a boiled Maine lobster with drawn butter, to a hearty bouillabaisse in the classic tradition of Marseilles, to a rich Coquilles St. Jacques.

Shellfish is the perfect appetizer or entrée for any occasion, formal banquet or late-night dinner for two.

Trout in Cream (not shown)
8 fresh trout, cleaned
1½ cups heavy cream
oil for brushing fish
salt and freshly ground pepper

1. Sprinkle the cavity of the trout with salt and pepper and brush heavily with oil. Brush a folding grill with oil. Place trout on grill over hot embers and cook for a minute or two on each side until skin is brown and bubbly.
2. Pour cream into a metal pan large enough to hold trout. Carefully place trout into the pan using tongs or spatula. Lay pan on the grill and cook for about 3 minutes on each side. Cream should be considerably reduced. Serve each trout on a plate and pour a bit of cream over fish. Serve immediately.

Note: Any small, whole fish, as long as it is fresh and there aren't too many bones, are perfect for this dish—small red snapper, small sea bass, porgies, sunfish, etc. A large whole fish, on the other hand, is best split open so that it lies flat on the grill, brushed liberally with oil, and cooked for 10–15 minutes on each side. Count on 1 pound of fish per serving and serve with fresh lemon.

Stir-Fried Shrimp with Broccoli
1 tablespoon cornstarch
2 tablespoons water
1 pound medium-sized shrimp, shelled and deveined
4 slices ginger, julienned
1 bunch broccoli, cut into pieces
¼ cup peanut oil
1 teaspoon sugar
1 tablespoon sherry
2 tablespoons good soy sauce

1. Combine cornstarch with water. Toss shrimp and ginger with cornstarch mixture.
2. Drop broccoli into boiling water and cook 1 minute. Drain.
3. Heat oil in wok or skillet and stir-fry shrimp until pink. Add broccoli, sugar, sherry and soy sauce and stir-fry about 1 minute longer. Serve.

Clams and Oysters Casino
(not shown)
24 soft- or hard-shell clams
24 oysters
Casino Butter (see page 90)

1. Scrub clams and oysters well.
2. Make the Casino Butter.
3. Open the clams and oysters or place the mollusks directly on the grill.
4. Discard top shell and lay mollusks in a flat pan. Cover each clam and oyster with a slice of Casino Butter and set the pan on the grill until butter melts.

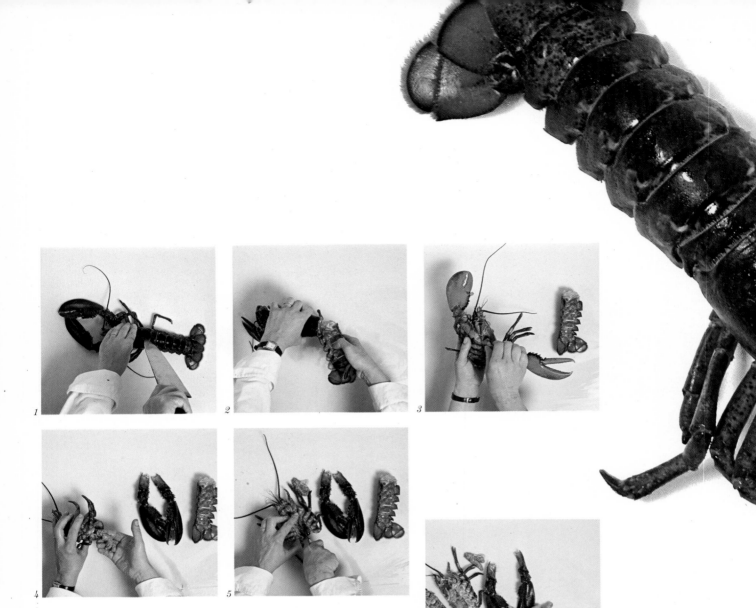

Cutting Lobster
1 lobster
1 very sharp medium sized knife

1. Kill the lobster by plunging the tip of the knife between the body and the tail. This severs the spinal cord and kills the lobster instantly, though the muscles will continue to twitch.
2. Twist the tail off lengthwise, or slice into chunks. Reserve the juice, the green tomally and the red coral, all of which can be added to the sauce.
3. Cut off the claws and divide at joints.
4. Cut the body in half and remove the gritty sand sac between the eyes. Lobster is now ready for cooking.

114

Lobster

Lobster Cantonese

¼ cup peanut oil
4 cloves garlic, chopped
2 tablespoons fermented black beans
¾ pound ground pork
4 one-pound lobsters, cut into serving pieces
1 cup chicken stock
8 slices fresh ginger, julienned
1 tablespoon sesame oil
1 tablespoon good quality soy sauce
4 scallions, chopped
1 tablespoon cornstarch
¼ cup water
3 eggs, beaten

1. Heat oil in a wok or a large skillet. Add garlic and black beans. Add ground pork and stir-fry about 3 minutes over high heat. Add pieces of lobster and stir-fry about 1 minute.
2. Add chicken stock and ginger slices. Cover. Cook about 5 minutes.
3. Add sesame oil, soy sauce, scallions, and cornstarch dissolved in water. Cook until mixture begins to thicken. Stir in egg and mix well.

Lobster Tails in Brandy Cream

2 lobster tails, with shells
2 tablespoons butter, melted
2 tablespoons brandy
¾ cup heavy cream
salt and freshly ground pepper to taste
2 scallions, julienned

1. Place lobster tails and butter in a saucepan. Cook, covered, for 15 minutes over a low flame.
2. Cool the lobster tails and remove the shells. Cut into slices and place the slices back in the pan.
3. Heat the brandy in a small saucepan. When hot, ignite with a match and pour the burning brandy over the lobster tails. When the flame dies down, stir in the heavy cream. Add salt and pepper to taste. Garnish with scallions.

Tomatoes Vinaigrette

6 large vine-ripened tomatoes, thinly sliced
9 tablespoons good olive oil
3 tablespoons best wine vinegar

2 tablespoons onion, finely chopped
4 tablespoons fresh herbs (parsley, tarragon, marjoram), finely chopped
Salt and freshly ground pepper to taste

1. Place the tomatoes in a salad bowl. Sprinkle each layer with the remaining ingredients.

Vegetable Terrine With Curry Mayonnaise (p. 85)

1 pound spinach, cooked and chopped
4 carrots, peeled and thinly sliced
3 white turnips, thinly sliced
1 package tiny frozen peas
1 quart defatted chicken stock
5 envelopes gelatin, dissolved in warm water
2–4 egg shells, crushed
1 tablespoon tarragon
2 egg whites, beaten until foamy
¼ cup Madeira
1 bunch scallions, finely sliced

1. Cook spinach, carrots, turnips and peas separately in chicken stock until tender (about 10 minutes for each vegetable).

2. Replenish stock as necessary to make 1 quart. Add the gelatin, egg shells, tarragon, and egg whites. Heat on a medium flame, stirring all the while, until mixture boils. Remove from heat. Strain the stock by pouring through a sieve lined with wet cheesecloth.

3. Add the Madeira and pour about ½ inch of liquid into a 1½-quart rectangular mold or terrine. Chill until firm.

4. Arrange a layer of carrot slices on the firm aspic. Add another layer of aspic, about ¼ inch thick. When this is set, add a layer of spinach, then more aspic, then another layer of vegetables, chilling between layers. Layer the vegetables by contrasting colors. Sprinkle the layer of peas with the scallion slices. End with a layer of aspic. Chill overnight.

5. To unmold, set terrine into very hot water and slide a sharp knife around sides of mold.

Cucumber Mousse

4 cucumbers, peeled
¼ cup chicken stock
2½ tablespoons (2½ packets) gelatin
¼ cup water
4 egg whites, beaten stiffly
2 cups heavy cream, beaten stiffly
½ bunch dill, finely chopped

1. Cook cucumbers in chicken stock until soft. Purée in blender and pass through sieve to remove seeds.
2. Dissolve gelatin in water and pour into hot cucumber mixture. Refrigerate until just beginning to set.
3. Fold in egg whites, cream, and dill and pour into a mold. Chill overnight.

Note: This makes a pale white-green mousse. For a stronger green color, add a few drops of green food coloring.

Brussels Sprouts with Chopped Almonds

2 pounds Brussels sprouts
4 tablespoons butter
1 cup almonds, coarsely chopped

1. Cook sprouts in boiling salted water, uncovered, until crunchy-tender. Test after 5 minutes by slicing one in half. Drain.
2. Toss with butter. Place in serving dish and sprinkle with almonds.

Grilled Tomatoes and Mushrooms (not shown)

4 large ripe tomatoes, halved
16 mushroom caps
3 tablespoons mustard (preferably Dijon-type)
3 tablespoons mayonnaise
½ cup butter, melted
salt and freshly ground pepper to taste

1. Place tomato halves, cut side up, and mushrooms, cap side up, on a cookie sheet.
2. Smear a spoonful of mustard and mayonnaise on each tomato half. Brush mushroom caps with melted butter.
3. Broil 10–15 minutes until tomato topping is sizzling. Season to taste.

Stir-Fried Vegetables

¼ cup oil
4 zucchini, quartered and cut into 2-inch lengths
1 pound string beans, topped, tailed, and parboiled
1 large onion, sliced
1 eggplant, cubed
2 red Bell peppers, cut in strips
2 green Bell peppers, cut in strips
1 pound cauliflower, broken into flowerets
salt and freshly ground pepper to taste

Heat oil in a wok or a large frying pan. When it is very hot, toss in all the vegetables. Toss, as you would a salad, for 2–3 minutes, being *very* careful not to overcook. Remember a certain amount of cooking will still go on after the vegetables have been removed from the heat.

Grilled Zucchini Halves

(not shown)
4 medium zucchini, halved
1 cup olive oil
3–4 garlic cloves, peeled
1 medium onion, coarsely chopped
2–3 dashes tabasco

1. Place oil, garlic, onion and tabasco in blender and blend until smooth. Marinate zucchini in this mixture, cut side down, for about an hour.
2. Place cut side down on grill and grill for 3–5 minutes. Turn over carefully with tongs and baste with marinade. Cook on uncut side another 3 minutes. Test for doneness—they should be slightly soft.

Snow Peas

2 tablespoons butter
1 tablespoon water
¼ pound snow peas, washed, topped and tailed

Melt the butter in a small saucepan. Add the water and snow peas.

Finger Sandwiches

1. Have on hand 2 loaves each of uncut white and brown bread. Bread must be at least 1 day old.
2. Butter and cream cheese must be at room temperature.
3. Prepare cucumbers by peeling and slicing as thinly as possible. Place in a large bowl and cover with salt. After two hours, rinse and pat dry.
4. Cover sandwiches with a damp linen towel to avoid drying out.

Cucumber Sandwiches

(about 20 sandwiches)
1 loaf uncut day-old bread
1 stick soft butter
4 cucumbers, peeled and sliced

1. Prepare cucumbers by peeling and slicing as thinly as possible. Place in a large bowl and cover with salt. After two hours, rinse and pat dry.
2. Slice off the heel of the bread. Spread the white portion of the bread thinly with butter. Then cut off a thin slice. Repeat until all bread is cut. Trim off crusts. Divide bread into halves.
3. Place several slices of cucumber on a piece of bread and cover with a second piece. Cucumber sandwiches can be made several hours ahead. Do not refrigerate. Place on tray and cover with a damp towel.

Cream Cheese and Radish Sandwiches

(about 20 sandwiches)
2 eight-ounce packages cream cheese
1 tablespoon Worcestershire sauce
4 tablespoons onion, finely minced
2 tablespoons mayonnaise
salt and freshly ground pepper
2 big bunches of radishes, trimmed and thinly sliced
1 loaf uncut day-old bread

1. Mix all ingredients except radishes and bread together. Taste and adjust seasonings.
2. Spread bread with some of the cream cheese mixture, then slice it, as explained under the cucumber sandwiches.
3. Arrange radish slices on the bread.

Cream Cheese and Olive Sandwiches

(about 20 sandwiches)
2 eight-ounce packages cream cheese
1 tablespoon Worcestershire sauce
4 tablespoons onion, finely minced
2 tablespoons mayonnaise
1 loaf uncut day-old bread
2 cups large pimento-stuffed olives, thinly sliced

1. Mix all ingredients except olives and bread.
2. Spread bread with some of the cream cheese mixture, then slice it, as you did with the cucumber sandwiches. Arrange olive slices on the bread.

Watercress Sandwiches
(about 20 sandwiches)
1 loaf uncut day-old bread
1 stick soft butter
2 bunches watercress

Use the same technique as for the
cucumber sandwiches. The
watercress sandwiches can be left
open-faced. Only the leaves of the
cress should be used.

Measurements

Measuring is an integral part of cooking, particularly baking, where the chemical reactions of the ingredients are crucial. Every kitchen needs some measuring devices to measure time and heat. The most basic tools are a set of measuring spoons (15), a set of dry measures for flour, where the contents can be evened with the top (10), and a liquid measuring cup with a pouring spout, preferably clear for easy visibility of the contents (1). With the changeover to the metric system, a beaker that includes both measurements (5) would be very handy. The same double marking is valuable on a scale. Although a scale isn't an absolute must, having one allows you to weigh a roast before cooking or to get an accurate proportion of flour and eggs in baking. Any baker would appreciate this scale (13); it allows you to put one ingredient in the bowl, then set the indicator back to zero so you can add another. You can do without a timer (11), but the time saved by not having to check on things and the food saved from burning make it a worthwhile investment for anyone. Thermometers are available for the oven (16), meat (17, 18), candy making and deep frying (14), among other things.

Potatoes and Rice

It has been estimated that half the world's population subsists wholly or partially on rice. With its high carbohydrate content, potatoes are a primary food of Western peoples, as well as a source of starch, flour, alcohol, and dextrin. They are diet staples the world over. Satisfying, nutritious, healthful and delicious, the incredible versatility of potatoes and rice makes them ideal candidates for any meal, from a ranch breakfast to an elegant formal supper. Preparation and presentation determine which dishes are suitable for each, but the potential is there.

Mashed Potatoes and Turnips

3 cups potatoes, peeled and quartered
3 cups yellow turnips, peeled and quartered
½-¾ cup heavy cream, heated
4 tablespooons butter
salt and pepper to taste

Boil turnips and potatoes together until tender (about 30 minutes). Drain. Pass through food mill. Season with the hot cream—stir in just enough to make desired consistency. Adjust seasoning with salt and pepper.

Boiled Red Potatoes with Dill

3 lbs. new potatoes
9 tbs. butter, melted
3 tbs. dill, chopped

1. Peel a strip from around the center of each potato.
2. Steam potatoes in a tightly covered sauce pan in a small amount of salted water, about 20-25 minutes, or until tender.
3. Drain, then briefly return pot to a low flame to dry off potatoes.
4. Toss in melted butter and sprinkle with dill before serving.

Roasted Russet Potatoes

4 large baking potatoes,
  quartered
4 tablespoons oil
salt and freshly ground pepper to
  taste
1 tablespoon chili powder

1. Rub the potatoes with salt,
   pepper and chili powder.
2. Sprinkle with oil and roast along
   with the beef. They should be
   done in 1 hour.

Salt-Roasted Potatoes

(not shown)
10 cups coarse salt
Enough water to make a paste of
  the salt
Lard to thickly coat the potatoes
8 baking potatoes

1. Add just enough water to the salt
   to make a thick paste.
2. Rub potatoes thickly with lard,
   then pat with the salt paste.
   When thoroughly coated, place
   directly in the embers and bake
   for about 1 hour. Each diner
   breaks the salt coating off before
   eating the potato.

Hashed Potatoes With Onions and Peppers

⅓ cup bacon fat or oil
1 large onion, coarsely chopped
6 cups potatoes, coarsely sliced
1 large red or green Bell pepper,
  thinly sliced
  salt and freshly ground pepper
  to taste
½ teaspoon sage, crumbled

Heat fat in a large skillet and add
onions. Cook until just turning
brown; then add potatoes and
peppers. Cover and cook over low
heat for 15 minutes, turning
occasionally. After 10 minutes,
add salt, pepper, and sage.
Potatoes should be tender.

Wild Rice with Pine Nuts

1 cup wild rice, soaked in water
  for 12 hours
2 cups chicken stock
¼ cup pine nuts
2 tablespoons parsley, chopped
¼ teaspoon rosemary, chopped
2 tablespoons Parmesan cheese
salt and freshly ground pepper to
  taste
Combine wild rice with boiling
chicken stock in an ovenproof pot.
Add pine nuts, parsley, and
rosemary. Cook for 35–40
minutes in 350° oven. Just before
serving, stir in Parmesan cheese
and seasonings. Toss well.

Pasta

Pasta was born in the Orient, but it was nurtured and refined by the Italians, with whom it has become synonymous. Today, as palates become more discerning (perhaps more educated is an apter way to describe it), the thick, rich, heavy Neapolitan tomato sauce that was for years the standard accompaniment to a plate of pasta is being replaced by sauces that are considerably more delicate: lightly cooked vegetables and cream, fish, herbs, the Oriental flavors of soy and ginger, whatever the local produce market and the imagination are capable of conjuring up. Match the pasta to your recipe: broad and sturdy for robust dishes, fine and light for the more delicate ones, curved or spiraled to capture the richness of one sauce, or straight for another, more refined, subtler sauce.

Vegetarian Delight

In *New American Cuisine*, fresh, crisp, colorful vegetables have achieved a dignity and stature all their own. While they still make a wonderful accompaniment to a main course, they are now served as the entrée itself. Make a hearty, savory pumpkin stew the star of your next supper. Or fix up a heaping platter of crunchy, delicious stir-fried vegetables. (Stir-frying is one of the best ways to cook vegetables. It preserves color, texture and flavor.) Or serve an elegant pesto, everyone's favorite. Should fresh basil be unavailable, here's a small secret: use fresh parsley instead. And if you're serving lamb try pesto prepared entirely with mint. Leave out the pine nuts but add a scant teaspoon of sugar.

Cold Vermicelli
1 pound cooked vermicelli
½ cup sesame oil
2 bunches scallions
½ cup soy sauce

Combine the ingredients. Serve cold.

Creamed Green Fettuccine
1 pound green fettuccine
8 tablespoons butter
8 tablespoons best-quality
  Parmesan cheese
½ cup heavy cream

1. Cook the fettuccine in boiling salted water for approximately 10 minutes. Drain.
2. Combine the butter, Parmesan and cream in a saucepan. Heat gently, then toss with fettuccine. Serve with extra Parmesan. Be sure it is of the best quality because it makes all the difference in this dish.

Pasta with Zucchini Pesto
Pesto
2½ pounds spaghetti
3 zucchini, cubed
2 tablespoons olive oil
4 tablespoons butter
¼ cup Parmesan cheese

2 cups basil leaves
1 cup Italian flat-leafed parsley
1 cup olive oil
¼ cup Parmesan cheese, grated
¼ cup pine nuts

1. Combine pesto ingredients in blender. The pine nuts should be folded in afterwards for texture.
2. Sauté zucchini in oil for 1 minute.
3. Cook spaghetti taking care

not to overcook. It should be "al dente"—firm to the teeth.
4. Toss the drained spaghetti with the butter and cheese and a few spoonfuls of the pesto. Serve on a platter with the zucchini sprinkled on top and a bowl of the pesto alongside.

A Vegetarian Supper
1. Old-Fashioned Carrot Custard Pie (p. 138)
2, 5, 6. Crudités with Curry Mayonnaise and Tomato Mayonnaise (p. 85)
4. Pumpkin Stew (p. 48)
7. Stir-Fried Vegetables (p. 124)
8. Quick and Beautiful Borscht (p. 47)
9. Caesar Salad (p. 71)
11. Pasta with Zucchini Pesto (p. 130)

Baking Pans

Baking is often as close to a science as to an art so don't try baking a cake in a different size or shape pan than the one specified unless you know how to compensate for the difference. You can certainly bake cookies on a jelly roll pan (18, 22) if you don't have a baking sheet (10, 24), or bake a quiche in an ordinary pie plate (4, 14, 16) rather than a quiche pan (2, 15, 20, 21, 27), but basically you'll want a pie in a pie plate and muffins in a muffin tin (7). In addition, there are loaf pans (6, 11, 12, 23) for breads and tea breads, square pans (8, 25, 30) for brownies, cakes and cookies, removable-bottom tart pans (19), layer cake pans (5), springform pans (1) for cheesecakes, pound and other tender cakes, pans (17) for shaped Kugel-hopfs and other molded

cakes, castiron cornsticks (26) and popover pans (9) and even an earthenware brick (13) for baking freeform loaves of bread on their own "hearth."

Because there is no direct heat in baking, materials are not as critical as for stove-top cooking. Aluminum and tinned steel are fine, but the heavier, professional pans cook better and last longer. Black steel seems to absorb heat more evenly, gives a golden crust and can shorten cooking time. Earthenware and ovenproof glass can be pretty as well as efficient. As long as the pan is of good quality, the choice of material is a matter of taste.

Baking Utensils

The frequent baker will need some tools to get the best results with the least effort: a cookie press (10), pastry blender (11), cookie cutter (17) and pastry bag (18). For baking pies and pastries, you'll need a pastry board. It can be wood, polyethylene, or marble like this one (1). Besides being beautiful, it stays cool, keeping the shortening in the pastry from melting while you work. But it needs a place of its own because it's too heavy to move about easily. The marble rolling pin (6) has the same qualities, but here the weight is an advantage, since it lets you use less of your energy

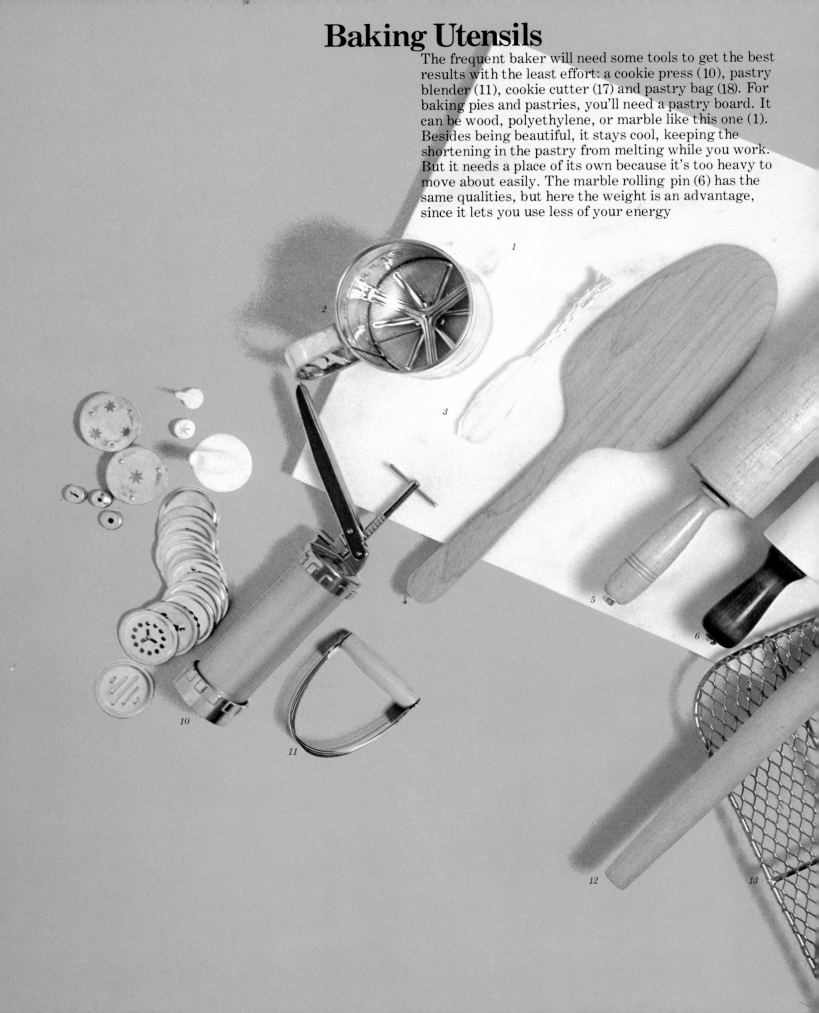

in rolling the dough—also true of the heavy wooden professional pin (5) with its ball-bearing action. For very tender dough the traditional French tapered pin allows you to "feel" what's happening better. A dough scraper (8,9), a pastry cutter (15) and brush (19) are handy accessories.

Whether it is bread, cookies or a cake, you'll need a cooling rack (13) to keep the bottom of the baked goods from getting soggy.

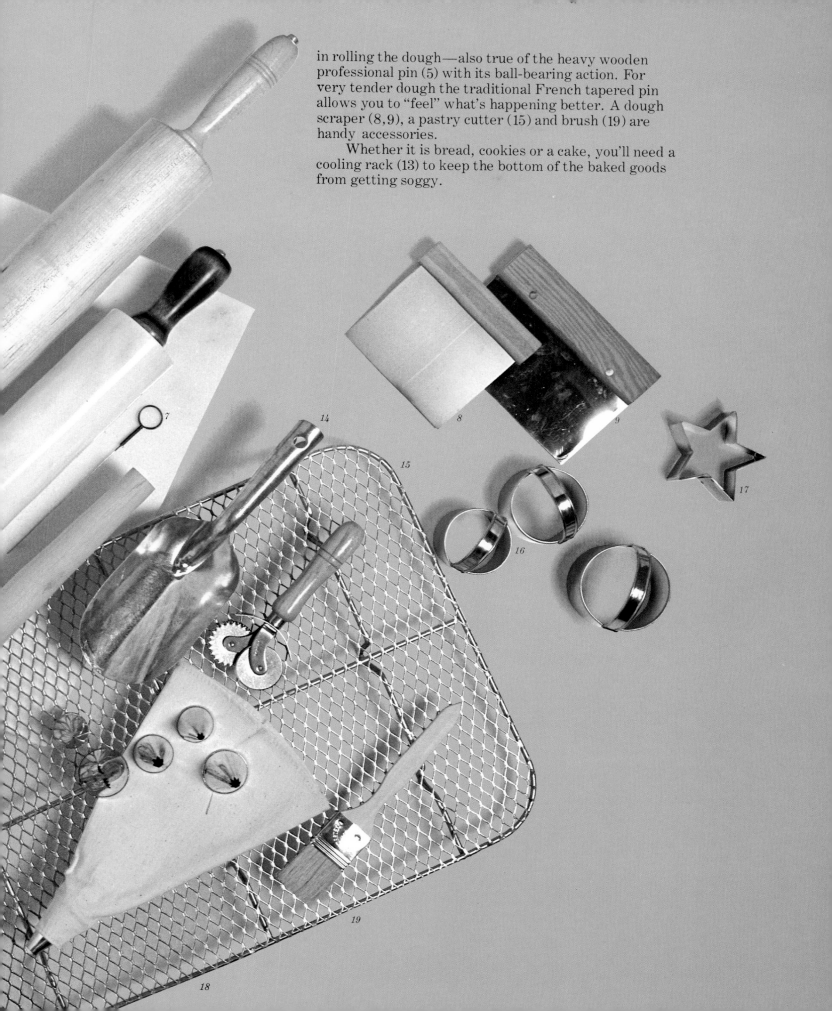

Pies and Cakes

Apple pie. Cherry pie. Pumpkin pie. Chocolate layer cake. Strawberry shortcake. Pecan pie. Pineapple upside-down cake. They are as American as ice cream. They require some care in preparation, for precise measurements yield the best results, yet they are all easy to make. With a little patience, anyone can create a flaky-crusted pie or a moist, tender cake to inspire praise from the most discerning of guests. The secret is in the ingredients—use only the best. You'll taste the difference...and so will everyone else.

Pumpkin Chiffon Pie

Graham cracker crust
1½ cups graham cracker crumbs
¾ cup butter, melted

Filling
2 teaspoons unflavored gelatin
¼ cup cold water
3 eggs separated
1¼ cups pumpkin, cooked and mashed
1 cup sugar
½ teaspoon cinnamon
¼ teaspoon allspice
¼ teaspoon nutmeg
½ teaspoon ginger
½ cup milk

Garnish
1-2 cups heavy cream, whipped

1. To make the pie shell, combine graham cracker crumbs and butter. Mix together and pat into a 9-inch pie shell. Chill for 10 minutes.
2. Soften gelatin in water (about 5 minutes).
3. Beat egg yolks with ½ cup sugar. Add pumpkin, spices, and milk. Cook over low heat, stirring constantly, until mixture begins to thicken (about 3-4 minutes).
4. Add gelatin mixture and cook another 2–3 minutes, until gelatin is dissolved. Cool for 30 minutes.
5. Beat egg whites until almost stiff and gradually add remaining sugar. Fold into the pumpkin mixture.
6. Pour filling into the pie shell and serve with whipped cream.

Old-Fashioned Carrot Custard Pie

Pie Crust
⅓ cup butter, melted
1 cup graham cracker crumbs

Filling
4 eggs, lightly beaten
¼ teaspoon salt
½ cup sugar
3 cups half-and-half, scalded
1 teaspoon vanilla
1 cup carrots, grated
1 teaspoon lemon extract

1. Combine butter and graham cracker crumbs and pat into a 9-inch pie shell.
2. Beat eggs, salt and sugar together. Beat in the scalded half-and-half. Add the vanilla and lemon extracts. Stir in the carrots.
3. Bake in a preheated 450° oven for 10 minutes. Reduce heat and bake at 325° for 30–40 minutes longer, until a knife inserted in the center comes out clean.

Apple Pie, Cheddared

Pastry
1½ cups flour
½ cup shortening
⅓ cup cheddar cheese, grated
3 tablespoons water

Filling
5 tart cooking apples, peeled and thinly sliced
1 cup apple sauce
1 teaspoon almond extract
½ teaspoon ground cinnamon
¼ teaspoon ground cloves
2 tablespoons sugar
½ cup cheddar cheese, grated

1. For pastry: Cut shortening into flour. Add water and cheese and knead into a ball. Let rest 30 minutes. Roll out pastry and pat

138

into a pie pan. Prick with fork, place foil on top, pat into place. Bake 15 minutes in a preheated 400° oven.
2. For filling: Combine apples, applesauce, spices, sugar and cheese. Stir well to mix thoroughly. Bake in a 350° oven for about 40 minutes.

Optional Crumb Topping for Apple Pie
½ cup flour
½ cup sugar
1 teaspoon cinnamon
⅓ cup butter

Mix dry ingredients together. Cut in butter until mixture is crumbly. Spread over fruit.

Buttermilk Blueberry Pancakes
2 cups buttermilk
1 egg, beaten
2½ cups flour
1¼ teaspoons soda
½ teaspoon salt
1 cup blueberries, fresh, frozen, or canned

Mix buttermilk and egg. Add flour, baking soda, and salt, stirring well to incorporate. Stir in drained blueberries. Cook on a greased griddle or in a frying pan. Serve with maple syrup.

Kugelhopf
1 package yeast
¼ cup lukewarm water
2 cups sifted flour
2 eggs
1 cup milk
⅓ cup butter
2 tablespoons sugar
½ teaspoon salt
1½ cups raisins

1. Soften yeast in water in a bowl. Stir in ½ cup of the flour and let it form a sponge. Then sift remaining flour over the sponge, cover with a towel and let the sponge rise through the flour. When it has risen, mix the flour in.
2. Beat in eggs, one at a time. Beat in milk and continue beating

until dough is smooth and elastic.
3. Cream the butter until light, then mix in thee sugar and salt. Stir butter mixture into dough. Then add raisins, mixing them in well. Turn dough into well-buttered kugelhopf mold and let rise in a warm place until doubled in bulk.
4. Bake in a 375° oven for 45 minutes or until done. Remove from mold and cool on a rack. When cool, dust with confectioner's sugar.

Pecan Pie
Pastry
1 cup flour
6 tablespoons butter
6 tablespoons vegetable shortening or lard
3 tablespoons sugar
2-3 tablespoons ice cold water

Filling
¼ cup butter
⅔ cup brown sugar, firmly packed
½ cup molasses
¼ cup honey
3 eggs, beaten
1 cup pecan halves

1. Make pie shell by cutting fat into flour. Add water and sugar. Knead briefly and let rest for 30 minutes.
2. Cream butter and brown sugar. Stir in remaining ingredients.
3. Bake in 450° preheated oven for 10 minutes. Reduce heat to 350° and bake 35-40 minutes longer.

Banana Bread
½ cup vegetable shortening
1 cup sugar
2 eggs
1 cup ripe banana, mashed
2 cups flour
3 teaspoons baking powder
1 teaspoon lemon juice
½ teaspoon salt
1 cup nuts, chopped (optional)

1. Have all ingredients at room temperature. Sift flour and baking powder together.
2. Cream shortening and sugar. Add beaten eggs, then stir in bananas and lemon juice.
3. Fold in flour mixture and nuts. Pour into a greased loaf pan and bake in a preheated 375° oven about 1 hour and 15 minutes.

Pound Cake
1 cup butter or margarine
1⅔ cups sugar
5 eggs
2 cups flour
1 teaspoon almond extract
2 teaspoons orange extract
1 cup candied fruit, cubed

1. Cream butter and sugar together. Beat in remaining ingredients. Pour mixture into a buttered and floured loaf pan.
2. Bake at 325° for 1½ hours.

Cookies and Sweets

Pastry, desserts and candies, consumed in modest amounts, can conclude a meal as appropriately as a period at the end of a beautiful sentence. As an accompaniment to coffee or tea, they are wonderful. You can opt for a sweet as nutritious as an oatmeal date bar or as sinfully rich as a chocolate truffle. If you serve something that is filling but small, your guests can indulge themselves without feelings of guilt later on.

Macaroons
(about 50 macaroons)
8 ounces almond paste
1 cup sugar
2 egg whites
½ teaspoon almond extract

1. Mix ingredients together, preferably in a machine.
2. Drop by spoonfuls onto a greased cookie sheet. Bake in a 300° oven about 1 hour.

Oatmeal Cookies
2 eggs
1 cup sugar
1 cup butter, melted
2 tablespoons maple syrup
1 teaspoon baking soda
1 teaspoon cinnamon
2 cups rolled oats
1 cup raisins
3 cups flour
¼ cup hot water

Beat eggs. Add other ingredients and mix well. Drop on a buttered baking sheet and flatten the cookies out. Bake for about 15 minutes in a 325° oven. Makes about 4 dozen.

Chocolate Roll
5 large eggs
1 cup sugar
6 oz. dark sweet chocolate
3 tablespoons cold water
Confectioner's sugar
1 cup heavy cream
1½ teaspoons vanilla
1½ teaspoons brandy

1. Separate eggs. Beat ¾ cup sugar into yokes until light and thick.
2. Over a low flame, melt chocolate in pan with the water, being careful not to burn it.
3. Cool chocolate slightly and fold with egg yolk mixture.
4. Beat whites until stiff and fold into chocolate mixture.
5. Butter baking sheet, line with waxed paper and butter again. Spread butter evenly over sheet.
6. Bake at 350° for 10 minutes, then at 325° for 5.
7. Remove from oven and cover top with damp dishcloth. Cool and place in refrigerator for 1 hour.
8. Carefully remove cloth. Dust a piece of waxed paper heavily with confectioners sugar and turn cake over onto paper. Carefully remove paper from top.
9. Whip cream until stiff and flavor with sugar, vanilla, and brandy to taste.
10. Spread roll with whipped cream and roll like a jelly roll.
11. Ice with Rich Chocolate Icing.

Rich Chocolate Icing
1 tablespoon butter
1 cup sugar
¼ cup milk
1 oz. bitter chocolate, melted
½ teaspoon vanilla, or to taste

1. Combine butter, sugar and milk and bring to boil, stirring constantly. Continue for 10 minutes.
2. Gradually add the melted chocolate, stirring constantly.
3. Remove from heat and beat until thick enough to spread. Add vanilla to taste.

New Orleans Pralines
(about 24 pralines)
2 cups light brown sugar
¼ cup butter
¼ cup water
2 cups small or broken pecans

1. Combine brown sugar, butter and water in a small saucepan. Set candy thermometer in pan before it begins to heat up. Cook over low heat, stirring constantly, until mixture boils.
2. Add the pecans. Cook until the temperature reaches the soft ball stage (248°).
3. Remove from heat and drop by spoonfuls onto a greased marble slab or a buttered cookie sheet.

Chocolate Mousse
8 eggs, separated
½ pound good quality chocolate
1 cup heavy cream
1 cup confectioner's sugar

1. Melt the chocolate in a double boiler.

2. Place in the container of your blender the egg yolks, chocolate, cream, and sugar and blend at lowest speed for a few minutes. Add the unbeaten whites and blend a minute or two longer.

3. Pour into individual containers and chill overnight. Serve in small quantities—this is very rich.

Fruits

Fruits have always been a light, refreshing dessert. They tend not to overstuff, yet are sweet and substantial enough to satisfy. The resurgence of interest in healthy natural foods has resulted in the increasing popularity of fruit dishes on the dinner party menu, from an exotic sliced kiwi to a tart, luscious baked apple laced with cinnamon. The growing popularity of exotic fruits from kiwis to mangoes to blood oranges has broadened the choice at the greengrocer.

Strawberries with Clotted Cream

3 boxes ripe strawberries
1 cup heavy cream
2 cups sour cream
1–2 tablespoons sugar

1. Hull strawberries but do not wash until just before serving; then wash and drain well.
2. Combine heavy cream and sour cream. Add sugar to taste.

Raspberries With Crème Anglaise

2 cups raspberries (do not wash)
3 egg yolks
½ cup sugar
1 cup light cream
1 tablespoon orange-flavored liqueur

1. Spoon raspberries into wine glasses, mugs, or your favorite container. Top with Creme Anglaise.
2. To make Creme Anglaise: Stir egg yolks with sugar until pale colored. Add the cream and stir constantly over moderate heat with a wooden spoon until thickened. If lumpy, strain. Stir in the orange liqueur.

Baked Apples With Heavy Cream

8 large baking apples, preferably Rome Beauty, cored
1 cup pecans, chopped
1 cup raisins
1 cup honey

Cinnamon
1 cup water
2 cups heavy cream, whipped

1. Place apples in roasting pan. Stuff with pecans and raisins. Pour on the honey and sprinkle with cinnamon.
2. Pour water into pan. Bake in a 400° oven for about 30 minutes or until soft. Serve at room temperature with cream.

Layered Fruit Bowl (not shown)

6 kiwi fruit, sliced
4 boxes strawberries, hulled and sliced
4 boxes blueberries
4 boxes raspberries

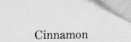

12 peaches, blanched, peeled, pitted, and thinly sliced
12 small purple plums, pitted and thinly sliced
lemon juice to taste
sugar to taste

1. Layer the fruit in a large glass bowl, sprinkling each layer with lemon juice and sugar. Cover and refrigerate for 1 hour. Do not prepare more than 2 hours ahead.

142

Tea

Tea was cultivated in China in prehistoric times and was probably first used as a vegetable relish (as it was in the American colonies and still is in some parts of the Orient), as well as medicinally, rather than as a beverage. Today it is used by more people and in greater quantity than any beverage except water. Too often we relegate tea to a light luncheon drink or the focus of a mid-afternoon snack. Yet tea is a beverage of endless versatility. As a brisk breakfast drink, tea can be as bracing and eye-opening as a cup of coffee. The subtle sweetness of Moroccan mint tea is a perfectly elegant accompaniment to a business or social occasion where something stronger would be a bit too much.

Black teas (pekoes, souchongs, congrous and the like) differ from green teas (imperials, gunpowders, hysons and so on) in having been fermented before firing. Oolongs, intermediate in color and flavor, are partially fermented. Green teas are produced primarily in China and Japan; black teas in China, Java, India and Ceylon; and oolongs in Formosa. The many kinds of tea are usually named for their color and grade, or for their district of origin, such as Darjeeling and Lapsang. The heavenly flavor results from volatile oils, the stimulating properties from caffeine, and the astringency from the tannin content.

The preparation of tea, while simple, is not taken lightly. It has been elevated to a ritual in Japan. The English insist that only a Briton can brew a proper cup. (Perhaps not without reason. Today the United Kingdom consumes nearly one-third of the approximately one million tons that are annually produced.) But the Moroccans, who take their tea brewing very seriously, would scoff at this. Whether they are right or wrong, you too, with a modicum of care, can successfully brew a delicious cup of tea. Rinse the pot out with boiling water Then add the tea leaves, pour boiling water over them, and let the mixture steep for a few minutes. That's all there is to it. You can use almost anything for the pot, from a modern glass design to a little Brown Betty, a fixture in every English home. If you're fixing tea for one, fill the tea infuser or egg with the leaves and steep it in your cup. It's as easy as using a tea bag, but the flavor you get is far better.

Coffee

Coffee is almost as old as civilization itself. It was known in Ethiopia before 1,000 A.D. Today, it is the second most valuable commodity in the world. Over ten billion pounds are produced each year, of which Americans drink one-third, some 450 million cups a day. Yet coffee remains a true bargain for gourmets. Even the most exotic beans can be had for less than a dime a cup when brewed at home. And coffee is available in a staggering variety of types, roasts and flavors. You can choose Bourbon Santos from Brazil; Celebes Kolossi from Indonesia; Tapuzza from Costa Rica; Harrar from Ethiopia; Indian Mysore; Columbian Maragogipe; Guatemalan Antigua; Papua New Guinea; Peaberry Cameroon; Sumatra Mandehling; Tanzanian Kilimanjaro; or Venezuelan Maracaibo, to name a few. You can purchase a slightly dark Viennese roast; a moderately dark French roast; a very black and oily Italian expresso; or a French chicory, a New Orleans favorite. A host of tantalizing flavors can now be readily found as well, naturally and evenly added while the freshly roasted beans are still warm—almond, cherry, chocolate, cinnamon, coconut, Jamaican rum, maple walnut, mint, and orange. Your selection can be brewed almost any way you like. You can percolate it as your mother undoubtedly did. You can drip it by hand through a plastic funnel lined with a filter. You can use an automatic drip coffee maker. You can use a

144

The After-Symphony Buffet

kitchen-sized electric expresso machine. All are designed to preserve the full, rich, natural aroma. Whatever the method used, the prime requirements are properly roasted, freshly ground coffee, freshly boiling water, and absolute cleanliness of utensils, as coffee is easily contaminated by foreign odors. Whether you want a simple cup for yourself or a quantity sufficient for a party of fifty-five, you will not lack for options in individual types, methods of brewing, and machines of sufficient capacity to meet the most demanding or expansive of needs.

A delicate, sophisticated Carpaccio to recall Scarlatti. A hearty, delightful creamed fettuccine, which would have warmed Verdi's heart. A light ballotine of chicken, if you are a serious cook. Poulenc would have approved. Remember that no one is really ravenous since the hour is late. And yet the ears have been blissfully charmed for the past two hours or three, and now the palette must be similarly wooed and won over. The menu should be subtle, elegant, orchestrated with care.

After-the-Symphony Buffet
1. Chocolate Roll (p. 140)
2. Boiled Red Potatoes with Dill (p. 128)
3. Creamed Green Fettuccine (p. 130)
4, 6. Stuffed Bass with Sauce Gribiche (p. 110)
9. Green Salad
11, 5. Ballottine of Chicken (p. 104) with Cumberland Sauce (p. 85)
13, 10. Carpaccio (p. 88) with Dill-Mustard Sauce (p. 84)

Silver and Glassware

There are hundreds of patterns from which to select and a complete array within each style. The classic patterns shown here are crystal from Schott-Zwiesel, and Queen Anne pattern silver.

Fortunately, open stock silver, glassware and china allows you to choose what you need initially and add to the basic set as the need arises.

A basic set of glasses: water goblet (6), red wine (4), white wine (3), and one or two bar glasses (8, 9). A basic place setting: knife (22), fork (18), teaspoon (28), salad fork (15), and butter knife (19). A cream soup (26) or bouillon (27) spoon and a place spoon might be the next additions.

Dinner for Two

It should be succulent. It should be sensual. And, above all it should be seductive. The meal should be prepared in advance. Only the finishing touches—the tossing of your veal and mushrooms in hot butter in the silver-lined bowl of a copper pan, for example—should be performed with a flourish on the spot. Keep in mind that the most exquisite of dinners can spoil the romance of the moment if you have to keep darting into the kitchen to peer beneath the lid of a simmering pot. On this particular occasion, let Eros, not Escoffier, be your guide.

Dinner For Two
3, 4. Raspberries with Crème Anglaise (p. 142)
7. Wild Rice with Pine Nuts (p. 129)
8. Lobster Tails in Brandy Cream (p. 115)
9. Veal Casino (p. 90)
10. Snow Peas (p. 124)
11. Raw Mushroom Salad (p. 69)

Credits

Page 37
Stainless steel skillet with heavy aluminum bottom sandwiched between two layers of stainless steel alloy. In 6 sizes from 6¼″ to 12½″. *Cuisinarts*

Page 38
1 Egg whisk with wooden handle. *Elofhans*
2 Egg turner of stainless steel, wooden handle. *Elofhans*
3 Two-speed egg beater of stainless steel. *Elofhans*
4 Solid copper bowl for beating egg whites. In 4 sizes from 8″ to 14″. *Hoan*
5 Balloon whisk with wooden handle. In 4 sizes from 10″ to 16″. *B.I.A. Cordon Bleu*
6 Ceramic egg separator from England. *H.A. Mack through Harriet Amanda Chapman*
7 Stainless steel egg poacher. *Manhattan Ad Hoc*

Page 39
1 Copper and brass chafing dish. *Ernest Sohn Creations*
2, 4, 5, 8, 9, 11 Contessa china Available in a wide range of pieces in green, yellow, black or red, outlined in black and trimmed with gold. *Ginori*

3 Copper and brass casserole server with ovenproof glass liner. *Ernest Sohn Creations*
6,7 Oyster crystal champagne glass and pitcher. *Wedgwood*

Page 45
1 Tin-lined copper tureen with brass handles. In 2 sizes, 4 qt. 14 oz. and 6 qts. *Charles F. LaMalle*
2 "Graniteware" porcelainized steel stockpot. *General Housewares Corp.*
3 Earthenware marmite. Available in several sizes. *Bazaar de la Cuisine*
4 Heavy hammered copper stockpot with cover, tin-lined. In 5 sizes from 9 qts. to 16 qts. *Charles F. LaMalle*
5 Extra-heavy hammered copper bain Marie with Limoges insert. *Charles F. LaMalle*
6 Brown flame-proof and oven-proof casserole. In 2 qts. or 4 qts. *Lauffer*
7 Valeska wine glass. *Schott-Zwiesel*
8 HiRise soup bowl and plate. Available in a range of colors. *Mikasa*
9 Walnut salt and peppermill set. *Charles F. LaMalle*
10 Heavy copper cocotte with cover and bronze handles, tin-lined. In 5 sizes from ¾ to 6¾ qts. *Charles F. LaMalle*
11 French willow cheese tray. *Williams-Sonoma*
12 Italian cheese cutter. *H.A. Mack through Harriet Amanda Chapman*
13 Granada stackable soup bowl and plate. *Villeroy and Boch*
14 Individual white porcelain ramekin. *Schiller & Asmus*
15 Terracotta plate. *Lee Bailey in Henri Bendel* Stainless steel flatware. *Frank McIntosh's Table Topping in Henri Bendel*
20 Boutique dishwasher safe soup bowl and plate. *Villeroy & Boch*
21 Ovenproof blue agate stoneware soup bowl and plate. *Bennington Potters*

Page 50
The Kitchen

Page 52
1 Commercial's extra-thick stockpot of nonstick, nonacid reacting Calphalon aluminum in 3 sizes from 8 qts. to 16 qts. *Manhattan Ad Hoc*
2 Porcelainized steel stockpot. *General Housewares Corp.*
3 Professional quality aluminum stockpot. Cover optional. In 8 sizes from 15 qts. to 100 qts.

Wear-Ever Food Service Equipment
4 SEB stainless steel pressure cooker with its own collapsible basket. In 3 sizes from 6⅓ qts. to 10½ qts. *Charles F. LaMalle*
5 Heavy hammered copper stockpot, tin-lined. In 5 sizes from 9 qts. to 16 qts. *Charles F. LaMalle*
6 Vollrath professional quality aluminum stockpot. Available in several sizes. *Manhattan Ad Hoc*
7 Cast-iron Dutch oven, 5 qt. capacity. *International Edge Tool Co.*
8 Heavy-gauge stainless steel covered saucepot, aluminum clad bottom. In 6 sizes from 4 qts. to 16 qts. *Farberware*
9 Marmite in stainless steel with "Thermo-radiant" bottom of aluminum sandwiched between 2 layers of stainless steel alloy. In 4 sizes from 2¾ qts. to 15½ qts. *Cuisinarts*
10 Aluminum vegetable steamer with adjustable steaming rack. *Hoan*

Page 53
1,6 Perforated and slotted French curved wooden spatulas. *H.A. Mack through Harriet Amanda Chapman*
2,7 Solid and slotted flat-edged wooden stirrers. *Harold Imports through Kellen & Co.*
3 Flexible rubber bottle and jar scraper with plastic handle. *Elofhans*
4,13,14 Set of rubber scrapers with wooden handles. *Rowoco through Kellen & Co.*
5 18/8 stainless steel serving spoon. *Lauffer*
8-12 Set of 5 wooden spoons. *Alfred E. Knobler*

Page 54
Seven-piece heavyweight

stainless steel kitchen utensil set. *Oxford Hall Silversmiths*

Page 55
1 Carbon steel griddle scraper with wooden handle. *Rowoco through Kellen & Co.*
2 Tinned wire skimmer. *H.A. Mack through Harriet Amanda Chapman*
3 Cook's fork with curved tines, maple handle, 14″ overall. *Forschner*
4,6 18/8 stainless steel slotted serving spoon and stuffing spoon *Lauffer*
5, 12 Heavy gauge stainless steel basting spoon and spatula. *Alfred E. Knobler*
7, 8 Stainless steel ladle and sauce spoon with dishwasher-safe compressed wood handles. *Cuisinarts*
9 Small sauce spoon with strainer lip. *Jane Products*
10 Off-set stainless steel spatula with wood handle. *H.A. Mack through Harriet Amanda Chapman*
11 Porcelain sauce spoon. *B.I.A. Cordon Bleu*

Pages 56–57
1 Bread knife of stainless steel. *H.A. Mack through Harriet Amanda Chapman*
2 Frozen food knife with stainless steel blade, Dura-wood handle. *J.A. Henckels*
3 High-carbon steel filleting knife with black wood handle, 7″ blade. *J.A. Henckels*
4 Stainless steel fish filleting knife with rosewood handle, 7″ blade. *Forschner*
5 All-purpose cleaver of carbon steel, rosewood handle, 7″, 8″, or 9″. *Forschner*
6 Stainless steel butcher knife with rosewood handle. In 5 sizes from 8″ to 14″. *Forschner*
7 Chrome-plated, magnetic butcher's steel. *J.A. Henckels*
8 Wusthof salmon slicer with stainless steel blade. *Manhattan Ad Hoc*
9 High carbon steel ham and roast beef slicer with hollow edge blade. *J.A. Henckels*
10 Ham and roast beef slicer with high carbon steel blade, Durawood handle. *J.A. Henckels*
11 Chef's 10″ slicing knife with high carbon steel blade, Durawood handle. *J.A. Henckels*
12 Carving fork with black Durawood handle, 7″ tines. *J.A. Henckels*

13 Chef's carving knife with 8″ high carbon steel blade, Durawood handle. *J.A. Henckels*

14,15,16 Chef's knives with 11″, 10″, and 8″ high carbon steel blades, Durawood handles. *J.A. Henckels*

17 Boning knife with narrow semiflexible stainless steel blade, rosewood handle. *Forschner*

18 Boning knife with wide heavy stiff blade of stainless steel, rosewood handle. *Forschner*

19 Chef's utility knife with 6″ high carbon steel blade, Durawood handle. *J.A. Henckels*

20 Stainless steel Sabatier utility knife with safety handle, 6″ blade. *Forschner*

21 Chef's paring knife with 4″ high carbon steel blade, Durawood handle. *J.A. Henckels*

Pages 64–65
Stainless steel barbecue tongs and spatula with wood handles. *B.I.A. Cordon Bleu*

Page 66
1 Galvanized tin tub. *Sun Glo*
3 White ceramic casserole. Microwave safe and ovenproof. In 3 sizes from 1 qt. to 3 qts. *Marsh Industries*
4 White ceramic bowl with thin red band. Available in other pieces and with blue band. *Conran's*
5,13 Stoneware crocks. Available in several sizes and shapes. *Jane Products*
6 White china cake stand. *The Pottery Barn* Individual white mousse dishes with red rim. Also available in a larger size and with blue or green rim. *Jane Products*
7 Wooden cheese box with cover. One of a set of 4. *Jane Products*
8 Self-stopping glass bottle. *Jane Products*
9 Beer glass. *Iittala USA Ltd.*
10 Earthenware marmite. Available in several sizes. *Bazaar de la Cuisine*
11 Red, white, and blue tattersall napkins. Conrans's
12, 14 Crockery bowl and pitcher. Bowl available in 4 sizes from 8″ to 15″. Pitcher available in 3 sizes from ¼ gallon to 1 gallon. Both available with blue or brown stripe. *Gaetano Pottery through A. Scafati*
15 French willow cheese tray. *Williams-Sonoma*
16 Blue and white enameled spoons. *Great North Woods*

Page 67
1 Spinning salad basket for drying greens, vegetables, fruits. *Rowoco through Kellen & Co.*
2 Olive oil can from Italy to keep oil fresh by keeping it away from air and light. Tinned steel with brass lid. 3 cup capacity. *Williams-Sonoma*
3 Olivewood salad servers. *Rowoco through Kellen & Co.*
4 Folding salad basket. *Hoan*
5 Wire salad basket. *Rowoco through Kellen & Co.*

Pages 72–73
1 Chopping bowl and chopper. *Manhattan Ad Hoc*
2 Maple cutting board, 1¾″ thick. Available in 4 sizes. *Hoan*
3 Stainless steel tomato knife. *Rowoco through Kellen & Co.*
4, 5 Lemon zester and lemon scorer. *B.I.A. Cordon Bleu*
6 French vegetable/fruit peeler for left or right hand. Stainless blade, aluminum handle. *Hoffritz*
7 Double melon baller. *Rowoco through Kellen & Co.*
8 All-purpose vegetable/fruit peeler in high impact plastic. *Alfred E. Knobler*
9 Flat cast-iron meat pounder for scallopini, chicken, pork. *Charles F. LaMalle*
10 Round brass meat pounder with upright handle. *Charles F. LaMalle*
11 Whip for quickly beating small amounts. Cherrywood handle. *Ekco*
12 Shaping knife with 2½″ curved stainless steel blade, wood handle. *Forschner*
13 Tomato slicer with cherrywood handle. *Ekco*
14 Wooden whisk. Will not scratch pots with nonstick linings. *Bazaar de la Cuisine*
15, 16 Stainless steel whisks, 8″ and 10″. *The Professional Kitchen*
17 Stainless steel whisk, 12″. *Hoan*
18 Tin whisk, 6″. *Hoan*
19 Stainless steel poultry shears from Italy, 9½″. *Hoffritz*
20 Italian half-moon chopper. Stainless steel blade, wood handles, 8″. *Hoffritz*
21 Potato masher with cherrywood handle. *Ekco*
22 Stainless steel grater-shredder. *International Edge Tool Co.*
23 Metal rotary grater for nuts, cheese, chocolate. *Charles F. LaMalle*
24 Self-cleaning garlic press. *Rowoco through Kellen & Co.*
25, 26 Italian zucchini and apple

corers. *H.A. Mack through Harriet Amanda Chapman*

Pages 76–77
1 French willow cheese tray. *Williams-Sonoma*
2, 4 Italian cheese knives. *H.A. Mack through Harriet Amanda Chapman*
3 Cousances cheese knife with beech handle. *Schiller & Asmus*
5 Italian cheese wedge. *H.A. Mack through Harriet Amanda Chapman*
6 Italian soft cheese slicer. *H.A. Mack through Harriet Amanda Chapman*
7 Cheese wire/slicer with rosewood handle. *Hoffritz*
8 Stainless steel cheese plane with teak handle. *Hoffritz*
9 Professional cheese wire. *International Edge Tool Co.*
10 Double-handled cheese knife. *Swissmart*
11 Set of 4 wooden cheese boxes. *Jane Products*
12 Glass cheese dome. *Jane Products*
13 Clay cheese brique to keep cheese fresh. *Cuisine Concepts*

Pages 80–81
1, 2 Reproduction of mid-19th-century American pressed glass pitcher (1 qt. capacity) and tumbler in Bellflower Pattern. *Metropolitan Museum of Art*
3, 14 Silver-plated platters. *Leonard Silverware*
6, 10, 11, 16 Delicately flowered Bianca china available in complete service. *Wedgwood*
12 Reproduction of an 18-century Ginori dish with stylized floral decoration. *Metropolitan Museum of Art*
13 Reproduction of a New England beaker, circa 1695. Silver plate. *Metropolitan Museum of Art*

Pages 82–83
1 Heavy hammered aluminum saucepan with iron handle. Cover optional. In 8 sizes from ¾ qt. to 12 qts. *Charles F. LaMalle*
2 Magnalite Professional saucepan with extra heavy bottom in all-aluminum alloy that will not interact chemically with foods, is easy to clean. In 1, 2, and 3 qt. sizes. *General Housewares Corp.*
3 Professional quality aluminum saucepan. Cover optional. In 2½ and 4½ qt. capacity. *Wear-Ever Food Service Equipment*
4 Bi-Metal professional saucepan of tri-layered steel heavily coated with copper. Cover optional. In various sizes. *Legion*
5 Hand-tinned copper saucepans with cast-iron handles. Lid optional. In 6 sizes from 1½ pts. to 4½ qts. *B.I.A. Cordon Bleu*
6 Le Creuset enameled saucepan in flame, yellow, spice brown, bluebell. In 4 sizes from 26 ozs. to 2½ qts. *Schiller & Asmus*
7 Stainless steel saucepan with heavy sandwiched aluminum bottom. Compressed wood handle. Lid optional. In 6 sizes from 2/3 qt. to 4 qts. *Cuisinarts*
8 Italian stainless steel saucepan with thick copper core in bottom for excellent heat conductivity. In several sizes. *Williams-Sonoma*
9 Heavy copper all-purpose pan with tin lining, riveted iron handle. In 8 sizes from 1½ pts. to 4¾ qts. *Charles F. LaMalle*
10 Enamel butter warmer, 1 pt. capacity. Available in red, white, brown, black. *Arabia*
11 Part of a 5-piece set of porcelain pans for melting butter, cooking sauces. In sizes from 12 oz. to 2 qts. *Charles F. LaMalle*
12, 13 Heavy hammered bain Marie with Limoges insert (1¾ qt. capacity) and copper vegetable steamer (3 qt. capacity). *Charles F. LaMalle*

14, 15 Stainless steel saucepan with aluminum clad bottom, 3 qts. Stainless double boiler and steamer inserts. *Farberware*

16 Cousances multifunction pan in enameled cast-iron. Top can be used as a skillet. In flame, yellow, brown, sienna, brownstone. In 1 qt. saucepan with 6½″ skillet top or 2 qt. saucepan with 8″ skillet top. *Schiller & Asmus*

17 Classic Pyrex double boiler. *Corning Glass Works*

Pages 86–87

1 Magnalite Professional baking pan in an aluminum alloy that does not interact chemically with foods, is easy to clean, 10″ x 13″. *General Housewares Corp.*

2 Heavy aluminum roasting pan. *Charles F. LaMalle*

3 Porcelained steel covered roaster in two sizes. *General Housewares Corp.*

4 Heavy cast-aluminum roaster with snug-fitting cover. *General Housewares Corp.*

5 Double-handled enameled covered roaster. Top can double as a low roasting pan. In several sizes. *Williams-Sonoma*

6 Open enameled roasting pan. *Bazaar de la Cuisine*

7 Professional aluminum roaster pan with reinforced steel straps, 16″ x 20″ x 24″. *Wear-Ever Food Service Equipment*

Pages 92–93

1 Tinned charlotte mold with lid in 8 sizes from 1 pt. to 2 qts. *B.I.A. Cordon Bleu*

2 Stainless steel colander in 4 sizes from 3 qts. to 18 qts. *Hoan*

3 All-purpose tinned wire basket for fruits, vegetables. *Charles F. LaMalle*

4 Crockery mixing bowls with blue or brown stripe. In 4 sizes from 8″ to 15″. *Gaetano Pottery through A. Scafati*.

5 Earthenware dough bowl. *Bon Jour through Kellen & Co.*

6 Set of wood-handled strainers. *Manhattan Ad Hoc*

7 Stainless steel mixing bowls. Available in 6 sizes from ¾ qt. to 13 qts. *Hoan*

8 English ovenproof mixing bowls with patented flat spot on bottom for easy tilting and beating. In 4 sizes. *Jane Products*

9 Sturdy Teflon roasting rack. *Williams-Sonoma*

10 Slanted wood knife block in natural. *Manhattan Ad Hoc*

11 Fluted Pyrex mold, oven-proof and microwave safe. *Corning Glass Works (Culinaria Collection)*

12 Plastic lidded stainless steel food storage containers. Set of 3. *Farberware*

13 Magnetic knife bar in 4 sizes from 8″ to 24″. *Rowoco through Kellen & Co.*

14 Purée sieve with Chinese hand from England. *H.A. Mack through Harriet Amanda Chapman*

15 Cast aluminium meat grinder with assorted cutting discs. *Bazaar de la Cuisine*

16 Nylon tamis sifter with wooden frame. In four sizes from 10″ to 16″. *Charles F. LaMalle*

17 Tinned steamed pudding mold in 3 sizes. *H.A. Mack through Harriet Amanda Chapman*

Pages 94–95

1 Extra-heavy round copper gratin pan. Tin lining and bronze handles. In 3 sizes from 5⅝″ to 12″ in diameter. *Charles F. LaMalle*

2 Stainless steel au gratin with heavy aluminum bottom sandwiched between 2 layers of stainless alloy. In 6 sizes from 6¼″ to 12½″. *Cuisinarts*

3 Large heavy aluminum paella pan, 15″ in diameter, cover optional. *Hoan*

4 Black iron paella pan with riveted iron handles. In 4 sizes from 12½″ to 17¾ in diameter. *Charles F. LaMalle*

5 Enameled cast-iron oval au gratin by Le Creuset. In 5 sizes from 8″ to 14½″. Flame, yellow, spice brown, blue. *Schiller & Asmus*

6 French porcelain oval au gratin. In 4 sizes from 8″ (individual) to 14″. *Hoan*

7 Contemporary enameled cast-iron oval dish by Le Creuset. In 4 sizes in black, brown, yellow, sienna. *Schiller & Asmus*

8 Tin lined oval copper au gratin. In 4 sizes from 10″ to 16″. *Bon Jour through Kellen & Co.*

9, 14 Clay nonstick, even-baking 10″ oval au gratin and 1½ qt. soufflé. *Copco*

10 Pillivuyt porcelain ramekins. Ovenproof, in sets of 6 in 5 oz. or 3½ oz. sizes. *Schiller & Asmus*

11 Oven-to-table Pillivuyt porcelain soufflé dish. In sizes from 1 pt. to 2½ qts. *Schiller & Asmus*

12 Ovenproof beige nappy for puddings. In two sizes. *Jane Products*

13 Round French ovenproof porcelain au gratin, 8½″ in diameter. *Bon Jour through Kellen & Co.*

14 White china shirred egg dish. In 2 sizes, 5⅝″ and 6⅞″ in diameter. *Charles F. LaMalle*

16 Enameled cast-iron lasagna pan, 3 qt. capacity. In red, yellow, brown, biscuit, blue. *Copco*

17 Nonstick clay baking dish. *Copco*

18 Glass lasagna dish for cooking or serving, 2½ qt. capacity. *Heller*

19 French earthenware rectangular platter or baking dish. In 3 sizes from 10″ to 14″. *Bon Jour through Kellen & Co.*

20 French china baking dish. In two sizes, 12″ x 8½″ or 14⅜″ x 10″. *Charles F. LaMalle*

21 Pyrex oval roaster for regular and microwave ovens. In 2 sizes *Corning Glass Works*

22 Unglazed earthenware baking dish from France. In 3 sizes from 12″ to 16¾″. *B.I.A. Cordon Bleu*

23 White Corning Ware open roaster, 12¼″ x 10¼″. *Corning Glass Works*

24, 25 Boda Nova heat-resistant glass gratin and soufflé dish, each with its own cork table mat. *Kosta Boda*

26 Low-sided rectangular baking pan of ovenproof Pyrex. In two sizes. *Corning Glass Works*

27 Baking and serving dish of hand-shaped and polished sand-cast aluminum alloy. Retains both heat and cold well. Hand wash. *Nambé*

28 Round ceramic baker with blue or brown stripe. In 4 sizes from 7″ to 15″ in diameter. *Gaetano Pottery through A. Scafati*

29, 30. *Manhattan Ad Hoc*

Pages 96–97

1 Gense covered casserole of 18/8 stainless steel with heavy copper bottom for better heat distribution when used on top of stove. Brass handles, 3½ qt. capacity. *Kosta Boda*

2 French earthenware marmite for slow simmering of soups and stews. Available in several sizes. *Bazaar de la Cuisine*

3 Handcrafted stoneware casserole for oven cooking only. In 2, 4, and 6 qt. sizes in white, natural, rust, or taupe. *Bennington Potters*

4 Brown stoneware casserole that can go from freezer to oven and even over direct flame. In 2- and 4-qt. sizes. *Lauffer*

5 Cousances round enameled cast-iron casserole. In 6 sizes from 1½ qts. to 9½ qts. in flame, brown, brownstone. *Schiller & Asmus*

6 Cousances Doufeu casserole of enameled cast iron. Fill indentation in top with ice cubes to hasten condensation of steam, which returns flavors to stew. In 3 sizes and same colors as #5. *Schiller & Asmus*

7 Ovenproof and microwave-safe white porcelain casserole. In 3½ and 4 qts. *Marsh Industries*

8 Enameled cast-iron casserole. In 4 sizes from 1½ qts. to 7 qts. in red, yellow, blue, biscuit, brown. *Copco*

9 Handcrafted blue agate stoneware casserole. In 3 sizes from 1 qt. to 4 qts. *Bennington Potters*

10 Unglazed clay cooker for meats, vegetables. In 3 sizes. *Cuisine Concepts*

11 Magnalite casserole of aluminum combined with magnesium for hardness and durability. 5 qt. capacity. *General Housewares Corp.*

12 Hand-shaped and polished casserole of sand-cast aluminum. Excellent heat retention for serving. In 3- and 4-qt. sizes. Hand wash. *Nambé*

13 Le Creuset enameled cast-iron oval casserole. In 3 sizes from 5 to 10 qts. in flame, blue, yellow, brown. *Schiller & Asmus*

14 Dual-purpose glass casserole. Top can be used as a gratin. Safe for oven or microwave cooking. In 1, 2, and 3 qts. *Heller*

6 Lobster and nut cracker, chrome-plated. *Rowoco through Kellen & Co.*
7 Shrimp peeler and deveiner. *International Edge Tool Co.*
8 Stainless steel fish tongs. *Rowoco through Kellen & Co.*
9 Oyster knife with stainless steel blade. *Forschner*
10 Heavy-duty clam knife with stainless steel blade. *Rowoco through Kellen & Co.*
11 Chrome-plated steel clam

15 Heavy copper cocotte with tin lining and brass handles. In 5 sizes from ¾ qt. to 6¾ qts. *Charles F. LaMalle*
16 White porcelain casserole for oven and microwave cooking. In 1, 2 and 3 qts. *Marsh Industries*
17 Flameproof ceramic cook-and-serve casserole. In a range of shapes and sizes from ⅓ qt. to 4½ qts. *Arabia*
18 Pillivuyt pâté terrine, 1-qt. capacity. *Schiller & Asmus*
19 Classic French white china casserole. In 4 sizes from 1½ pts. to 2 qts. *B.I.A. Cordon Bleu*
20 Italian stainless steel casserole with thick copper core built into the bottom for better heat conduction. In 3- and 5½-qt. sizes. *Williams-Sonoma*

Pages 100–101
4 Lead crystal goblets, 8 oz. Reproduction of American mid-19th-century Bellflower Pattern pressed glass. *Metropolitan Museum of Art*
5 Copy of early 19th-century blown three-mold decanter, 28 oz. capacity. Also available in amber. *Metropolitan Museum of Art*
7,10 From a collection of "Famille Verte" porcelain, a design in the tradition of prized Chinese pieces of the K'ang-hsi period, 1662–1722. *Metropolitan Museum of Art*
13 Reproduction of early 19th-century American bowl Blown 3-mold glass in quilted diamond pattern. *Metropolitan Museum of Art*

Page 105
1 A kitchen machine whose standard hardworking whipper, beater, and dough hook can be augmented by optional attachments like grinders, puree attachments and a food processing kit that will chop, grate, slice and julienne. *Kitchen Aid*
2. Copper lining bowl for

KitchenAid *Atlas Metal Spinning Co. through Kellen & Co.*
3, 4 Food processor with extra-large bowl and the capacity to chop, slice, grate, puree, knead dough. Optional blade for thin or thick slices, julienning, etc. and an expanded feed tube to let you slice whole small to medium-sized fruits and vegetables. *Cuisinart*

Pages 106–107
1 Automatic icecream maker that fits in the freezer and eliminates the need for salt and ice. *Salton*
2 Juice extractor for fresh juice from noncitrus fruits or vegetables in seconds. *Braun USA*
3 Automatic waffle baker with nonstick removable grids that reverse for open or closed grilling. *General Electric*
4 Simple chrome 4-slice toaster. *Toastmaster*
5 SEB toaster with an opening big enough for slices of French bread. *Manhattan Ad Hoc*
6 Hand mixer with beater ejector and heel rest, 3 speeds. *General Electric*
7 Electric pasta machine from Italy with adjustable kneading-rolling attachment and wide and narrow cutting rollers. *Hammacher Schlemmer*
8 Double-duty Cousances deep fryer-slow cooker. Aluminum fry basket and Teflon interior for easy cleaning. Optional crockery pot insert for extra slow cooking. *Schiller & Asmus*
9 Powerful professional bar-model blender with simple on-off switch. *Waring*
10 Automatic citrus juicer starts operating when pressure is applied. *Braun USA*
11 Stainless steel broiler-rotisserie for smokeless cooking of steaks, chops or large roasts. Disassembles for easy cleaning and storage. Shish-Kebab accessory optional. *Farberware*

12 Polished aluminum skillet for every kind of cooking from frying to stewing without heating up the stove. Easy cleaning. *General Electric*

Pages 108–109
2 White Corningware pie plate, 9". *Corning Glass Works*
4 White ceramic candlestick. In 2 sizes. *Manhattan Ad Hoc*
8 Stoneware ovenproof soup bowl. *Lauffer*
9,11 Sans Souci white china. Available in a complete range of dining and serving pieces. *Rosenthal USA*
12 Individual white porcelain ramekin. *Schiller & Asmus*

Page 112
1 Römertopf clay fish cooker for fatless cooking. *Reco International*
2 Tinned fish poacher with rack. In 4 sizes. *Charles F. LaMalle*
3 Wire fish grill for use over an open fire. In 16" and 20" sizes. *B.I.A. Cordon Bleu*
4 Heavy gauge aluminum fryer-steamer with steel mesh basket and steaming rack, 20-qt. capacity. *Leyse*
5 Lobster cracker. *Charles F. LaMalle*

opener with stainless blade. *Hoffritz*
12 Fish scaler from Sweden, 18/8 stainless steel. *Elofhans*
13 Fish knife and scaler. *Rowoco through Kellen & Co.*

Page 117
1 Deluxe wok set, including 14" steel wok with cover and cooking ring, deep-fry skimmer, cleaning brush, stainless steel ladle and spatula, cooking chopsticks and steam rack. All packaged in a wooden box with wok cookbook. *Taylor & Ng*
2 Lightweight aluminum steampot with multiple tiers. Steam trays can also be used in wok. In 10" or 12" diameter. *Taylor & Ng*
3 Tightly woven Chinese steamer to use with wok, 10" diameter. *Alfred E. Knobler*
4 Flat-bottom wok with single wooden handle. In heavy-gauge steel with aluminum cover. *Taylor & Ng*
5 Portable chrome burner, fueled with denatured alcohol. *Taylor & Ng*
6,7,8 Chinese cleavers for mincing (6), slicing (7), and chopping (8). Carbon steel blades, wooden handles. *Taylor & Ng*

18 Black steel jelly roll pan. *Manhattan Ad Hoc*
19 Tin tart pan with removable bottom. In 4 sizes from 8" to 13". *Rowoco through Kellen & Co.*
20 Clay nonstick quiche pan. *Copco*
21 French porcelain quiche pan. In 8", 9", or 10". *Bon Jour through Kellen & Co.*
22 Aluminum all-purpose baking pan, 15½" x 10½". *Wear-Ever Aluminum*
23 Pyrex loaf pan in 1½ and 2 qt. sizes. *Corning Glass Works*
24 Blue steel baking sheet, 16" x 12" or 20" x 13". *B.I.A. Cordon Bleu*
25 Square clay nonstick baking dish for cakes or brownies. *Copco*
26 Cast-iron cornstick pan. *General Housewares Corp.*
27 Cousances black cast-iron quiche pan, 10¼". *Schiller & Asmus*
30 Square aluminum baking pan, 8" x 8" or 9" x 9". *Wear-Ever Aluminum*

Pages 136–137
1 Marble pastry board. Available in 5 sizes, various colors. *Vermont Marble*
2 Sturdy 2-cup flour sifter. *Manhattan Ad Hoc*
3 Feather pastry brush. *Manhattan Ad Hoc*
4 Birch oven peel from France. *H.A. Mack through Harriet Amanda Chapman*
5 Professional ball-bearing rolling pin, available in several sizes. *The Professional Kitchen*
7 Cake tester. *Hoan*
8 Stainless steel dough scraper. *Rowoco through Kellen & Co.*
9 Pasta scraper. *Hoan*
10 Swedish cookie press for up to 24 different shapes of cookies. Attachments to fill cream puffs, etc. *Elofhans*
11 Pastry blender. *Rowoco through Kellen & Co.*
12 Tapered French rolling pin. *Manhattan Ad Hoc*
13 Nickel-plated cooling rack. In 4 sizes. *Rowoco thrugh Kellen & Co.*
14 Tin flour scoop. *Hoan*
15 Double pastry cutter, with plain and fluted edge. *Professional Kitchen*
16 Biscuit cutters, set of 3. *Jane Products*
17 Cookie cutter available in many shapes. *The Professional Kitchen*
18 Pastry bag and tubes for decorating cakes. *Charles F. LaMalle*

19 Pastry brush from Germany. In 1" and 1½" sizes. *H.A. Mack through Harriet Amanda Chapman*

Page 143
1 Stainless steel tea kettle, 1½ qt. capacity. *Farberware*
2 Enameled cast-iron tea kettle, 2½ qt. capacity. Available in red, blue, yellow, brown, biscuit. *Copco*
3 White stoneware teapot, available with matching mugs. *Rubel & Co.*
4 White ceramic tea egg. *Bazaar de la Cuisine*
5 Stainless steel tea strainer. *Hoan*
6 Stainless steel infuser. *H.A. Mack through Harriet Amanda Chapman*
7 Brown Betty teapot for tea in the English manner. *Alfred E. Knobler*
8 Boda Nova heat-resistant glass teapot with its own warmer. *Kosta Boda*

Pages 144–145
1 Stainless steel one-cup drip coffee maker. *Bazaar de la Cuisine*
2 Automatic drip filter coffee maker with Dial-A-Brew control to let you regulate the strength of the coffee. Large size brews 12 cups, small size 10. Either can brew as few as 3 successfully. *Norelco*
3 All-automatic stainless steel coffee maker for a large party. It brews 12-55 cups of coffee and keeps it at ideal serving temperature. *Farberware*
4 A minigrinder for grinding your own coffee beans just before brewing. Grinds enough for 10 cups quickly, easily. *Braun USA*
5 The classic French Melior. Simple to operate and easily adapted to produce the strong coffee the French drink—or a weaker brew if you prefer. *Bon Jour through Kellen & Co.*
6 A handsome machine that can quickly provide 2-8 cups of espresso or cappuccino or 2-4 cups of filter coffee with just a twist of the dial. *Salton*
7 Aluminum espresso pot from Italy, 12 cups. Also available for 3, 6 and 9 cups. *Hoan*
8 Aluminum stove-top espresso and cappuccino maker, 6 cups. *Bloomingdale*

Pages 146–147
1 Small silver-plated rectangular tray. *WMF of America*

3 Silver-plated covered vegetable dish from Italy. *A & S Olive*
4 Rectangular Chippendale tray in silver plate. *WMF of America*
5,6,9,10 Glass bowls in traditional Paul Revere shape. Small bowls 6" in diameter. Salad bowl 10" in diameter. *Pilgrim Glass*
7,8 Ashford cut crystal decanter and wine glasses. *Wedgwood*
11 Round Chippendale tray in silver plate. *WMF of America*
12 Blue Wheat china. Available in a complete range of pieces. *Coalport*
13 Silver-plated oval platter from Italy. *A & S Olive*

Pages 148–149
All crystal from Schott-Zwiesel.
1 Meran port glass.
2 Meran champagne flute.
3 Meran white wine.
4 Meran red wine.
5 Meran iced tea.
6 Meran water goblet.
7 Benedikt beer mug.
8 Cannes highball.
9 Cannes oldfashioned.
10 Meran sherry.
11 Meran liqueur.
12 12½ oz. brandy.

Sterling silver in Queen Anne pattern from Cooper Brothers.
14 Oyster fork.
15 Salad fork.
16 Fish fork.
17 Luncheon fork.
18 Dinner fork.
19 Butter knife.
20 Fish knife.
21 Luncheon knife.
22 Dinner knife.
23 Serving spoon.
24 Iced tea spoon.
25 Place spoon.
26 Cream soup spoon.

27 Bouillion spoon.
28 Teaspoon.
29 Demitasse spoon.

Page 150
1 Faceted Italian glass espresso cups. *Bormioli*
2 Silver-plated candlesticks. *WMF of America*
3 Long-stemmed glass fruit bowl. *Colony*
4 Glass bowl in classic Paul Revere shape, 6". *Pilgrim Glass*

5 Reflection crystal champagne flutes. *WMF of America*
6 Glass vase available in a range of sizes. *Colony*
7,8,9 Heavy silver-plated serving dishes from Italy. *A & S Olive*
10 Art deco bowl, 12". *Pilgrim Glass*
12 Octagonal plate in heavy silver plate from Italy. *A & S Olive*
13 Black plastic and stainless steel flatware designed by Larry Laslo. *Mikasa*

Index of Manufacturers

Akron Leonard 1418 Kitchen
1418 Third Avenue
New York, NY 10021
(212) 794-1080

Arabia of Finland
Div. of Wartsila Inc.
5603 Howard Street
Niles, IL 60648
(312) 647-9650

Atlas Metal Spinning Co.
183 Beacon Street
South San Francisco, CA 94080
(415) 871-6710

Bazaar de la Cuisine Inc.
(Retail Store)
1003 Second Avenue
New York, NY 10022
(212) 421-8028

Bennington Potters, Inc.
324 County Street
Bennington, VT 05201
(802) 447-7531

B.I.A. Cordon Bleu
375 Quarry Rd.
Belmont, CA 94002
(415) 595-2400

Bon Jour Imports Corp.
P.O. Box AD
Horsham, PA 19044
(215) 674-5930

Bormioli Glass Inc.
230 Fifth Avenue
New York, NY 10001
(212) 889-5849

Braun Appliances, USA
55 Cambridge Parkway
Cambridge, MA 02142
(617) 492-2100

Charles F. Lamalle, Importer
1123 Broadway
New York, NY 10010
(212) 242-0750

Chemex Corporation
P.O. Box 897
Pittsfield, MA 01201
(413) 499-2370

Colony Glassware
1115 Broadway
New York, NY 10010
(212) 924-7700

Commercial Aluminum
Cookware Co.
P.O. Box 583
Toledo, OH 43693
(419) 666-8700

Conran's (Retail Store)
160 East 54th Street
New York, NY 10022
(212) 371-2225

Coalport
41 Madison Avenue
New York, NY 10010
(212) 532-5950

Copco Inc.
50 Enterprise Avenue
Secaucus, NJ 07094
(212) 889-4500

Cooper Brothers
Sheffield, England
(At leading stores in USA)

Corning Glass Works
Consumer Products Division
Corning, NY 14830
(607) 974-9000

Cousances
(See Schiller & Asmus)

Cuisinarts, Inc.
411 West Putnam Ave.
Greenwich, CT 06830

Cuisine Concepts
13477 12th Street
Chino, CA 91710
(714) 591-3813

Ekco Housewares Co.
9234 West Belmont Avenue
Franklin Park, IL 60131
(609) 448-5630

Elofhans Products, Inc.
234 Westport Avenue
Norwalk, CT 06851
(203) 847-4555

Ernest Sohn Creations
Housewares/Giftwares Div.
American Trading & Production Corp.
880 East 72nd Street
Cleveland, OH 44103
(216) 361-2922

Farberware®
Subsidiary of Walter Kidde & Co., Inc.
1500 Bassett Avenue
Bronx, NY 10461
(212) 863-8000

R.H. Forschner Co., Inc.
828 Bridgeport Avenue
Shelton, CT 06484
(203) 929-6391

Frank McIntosh's Table
Topping at Henri Bendel
10 W. 57th Street
New York, NY 10019
(212) 247-1100

Gaetano Pottery of
California, Inc.
10675 Hickson
El Monte, CA 91731
(213) 442-2858

General Electric Co.
Housewares & Audio
Business Div.
Bridgeport, CT 06602
(203) 382-2229

General Housewares Corp.
P.O. Box 4066
Terre Haute, IN 47804
(812) 234-3739

Ginori
711 Fifth Avenue
New York, NY 10022
(212) 752-8790

Gourmet Ltd.
376 East St. Charles Rd.
Lombard, IL 60148
(312) 627-1666

Great North Woods
(Retail Store)
425 Fifth Avenue
New York, NY
(212) 889-0983

Hammacher Schlemmer
147 E. 57th Street
New York, NY
(212) 421-9000

Harriet Amanda Chapman, Inc.
225 Fifth Avenue
New York, NY 10010
(212) MU 3-2647

Heller Designs, Inc.
41 Madison Avenue
New York, NY 10010
(212) 685-4200

J.A. Henckels
Zwillingswerk, Inc.
1 Westchester Plaza, Box 127
Elmsford, NY 10523
(914) 592-7370

Hoan Housewares
615 East Crescent Ave.
Ramsey, NJ 07446
(201) 825-0900

Hoffritz
515 West 24th St.
New York, NY 10011
(212) 924-7300

Iittala USA Ltd.
225 Fifth Avenue
New York, NY 10010
(212) 689-7430

International Edge Tool Co.
565 Eagle Rock Ave.
Roseland, NJ 07068
(201) 228-5300

Jane Products, Inc.
40 West 86th Street
New York, NY 10024
(212) 677-1636

Kellen & Co.
225 Fifth Avenue
New York, NY 10010
(212) 532-8093

The Kitchen
(See Akron Leonard
1418 Kitchen)

Kitchen Aid Division
Hobart Corp.
Troy, OH 45374
(513) 355-7171

Alfred E. Knobler & Co., Inc.
Moonachie, NJ 07074
(212) 564-8784

Kosta Boda USA Ltd.
225 Fifth Avenue
New York, NY 10010
(212) 679-2280

H.E. Lauffer Co., Inc.
Belmont Drive
Somerset, NJ 08873
(201) 356-7676

Le Creuset
(See Schiller & Asmus, Inc.)

Lee Bailey at Henri Bendel
10 W. 57th Street
New York, NY 10019
(212) 247-1100

Legion Utensils Co., Inc.
P.O. Box 698
Waynesboro, GA 30830
(404) 738-9667

Leonard Silver Mfg. Co. Inc
225 Fifth Avenue
New York, NY 10010
(212) 725-1550

Leyse Aluminum Co.
Kewaunee, WI 54216
(414) 388-3111

L'Herbier de Provence
156 E. 64th Street
New York, NY 10021
(212) 759-8240

H.A. Mack & Co., Inc.
165 Newbury Street
Boston, MA 02116
(617) 266-2630

Manhattan Ad Hoc (Retail
Store)
842 Lexington Ave
New York, NY 10021
(212) 752-5488

Marsh Industries
1224 East 28th Street
Los Angeles, CA 90011
(213) 233-4393

Mazer Store Equipment Co.,
Inc.
207 Bowery
New York, NY 10002
(212) 674-3450

The Metropolitan Museum of
Art
Fifth Avenue at 82nd St.,
New York, NY 10028
Mail Order: 255 Gracie Station
New York, NY 10028
(212) 758-8991

Mikasa
25 Enterprise Avenue
Secaucus, NJ 07094
(201) 867-9210

Nambé Mills
301 E. Alameda
Santa Fe, NM 87501
(505) 988-5526

Norelco
Consumer Products Div.
100 East 42nd Street
New York, NY 10017
(212) 683-6082

A & S Olive Inc.
225 Fifth Avenue
New York, NY 10010
(212) 683-6082

Oxford Hall Silversmiths, Inc.
225 Fifth Avenue
New York, NY 10010
(212) 686-3223

Pasta & Cheese (Retail Store)
1375 Third Avenue
New York, NY 10021
(212) 988-0997
(and other locations throughout
New York City)

Pilgrim Glass Corp.
Moonachie, NJ 07074
(201) 641-2600

Pillivuyt
(See Schiller & Asmus)

The Pottery Barn
117 East 59th Street
New York, NY 10022
(212) 741-9132

The Professional Kitchen
18 Cooper Square
New York, NY 10003
(212) 254-9000

Reco International Corp.
138-150 Haven Avenue
Port Washington, NY 11050
(516) 767-2400

Richard S. Smith, Inc.
225 Fifth Avenue
New York, NY 10010
(212) 684-2250

Rosenthal USA Ltd.
411 East 76th Street
New York, NY 10021
(212) 570-4600

Rowoco
700 Waverly Avenue
Mamaroneck, NY 10543
(914) 698-4002

Rubel & Company
225 Fifth Avenue
New York, NY 10010
(212) 683-4400

Salton, Inc.
1260 Zerega Avenue
Bronx, NY 10462
(212) 931-3900

Scafati & Co.
101 E. Highland Avenue
Atlantic Highlands, NJ 07716
(201) 291-9325

Schiller & Asmus, Inc.
1525 Merchandise Mart
Chicago, IL 60654
(312) 644-7747

Schott-Zwiesel Glass, Inc.
11 East 26th Street
New York, NY 10010
(212) 689-5560

Sun Glo Corp.
P.O. Box 348
Chappaqua, NY 10514
(914) 238-5111

Swissmart, Inc.
444 Madison Avenue
New York, NY 10022
(212) 751-3768

Taylor & Ng
400 Valley Drive
Brisbane, CA 94005
(415) 467-2600

Terraillon
950 South Hoffman Lane
Central Islip, NY 11722
(516) 582-4747

Toastmaster Div.
1801 North Stadium Blvd.
Columbia, MO 65201
(314) 445-8666

Vermont Marble Co.
Proctor, VT 05765
(800) 451-4468

Vermont Soapstone Co.
Perkinsville, VT 05151
(802) 263-5404

Villeroy & Boch Tableware Ltd
41 Madison Avenue
New York, NY 10010
(212) 683-1747

Waring Products
New Hartford, CT 06057
(203) 379-0731

Wear-Ever Food Service
Equipment
1111 No. Hadley Road
Fort Wayne IN 46801
(219) 432-9511

Wear-Ever Aluminum, Inc.
Chilicothe, OH 45601
(614) 775-9100

Wedgwood
Wedgwood Plaza
Lyndhurst, NJ 07071
(201) 460-9200

Williams-Sonoma Inc. (Retail Store)
P.O. Box 3792
San Francisco, CA 94119
(415) 982-4720

WMF
85 Price Parkway
Farmingdale, NY 11735
(516) 293-3990